REMEMBERING THE STOP THE SEVENTY TOUR
CAMPAIGN

Geoff Brown & Christian Høgsbjerg

Foreword by Peter Hain

a Redwords pamphlet

Apartheid is not a game: Remembering the Stop the Seventy Tour Campaign by Geoff Brown and Christian Høgsbjerg

Foreword by Peter Hain

a Redwords pamphlet published January 2020

ISBN: 978-1-912926-58-9
ebook: 978-1-912926-60-2
kindle: 978-1-912926-59-6

Redwords is connected to
Bookmarks: The Socialist Bookshop, 1 Bloomsbury Street,
London WC1B 3QE
https://bookmarksbookshop.co.uk

Design and production: Roger Huddle
Printed by Halstan & Co., Amersham

Cover: Sharpeville massacre 1960
Half title: South African Children demonstate against apartheid
Title: Anti-Apartheid demonstration

Leicester protest at Welford Road 1969

APARTHEID IS NOT A GAME

ACKNOWLEDGEMENTS

With very many thanks to all those who shared their memories of campaigning and helped us with this pamphlet in various ways, but particular thanks must go to Sue Arnall, Peter Binns, Ian Birchall, Tony Collins, John Creaby, Andrew Drummond, Kath Eilbeck, Michael Farrell, Fred Fitton, Lindsey German, Tony Goodchild, John Gray, Christabel Gurney, Martin Gleeson, Peter Hain, Paul Holborow, Roger Huddle, Ronnie Kasrils, Ken Keable, Jim Kincaid, Sally Kincaid, Gary Lewis, Pete Loewenstein, Bob Newland, Jim Nichol, Anna Paczuska, Tom Pendry, Huw Pudner, David Purdy, Margaret Renn, Jeannie Robinson, Europe Singh, John Sturrock, Janet Whelan and the staff of the Borthwick Institute for Archives, University of York (which houses the Dennis Brutus Archive) and the archive of the Anti-Apartheid Movement, Bodleian Library, University of Oxford.

FOREWORD PETER HAIN

When around 100,000 British anti-apartheid activists mobilised to disrupt and wreck a planned all-white South African cricket tour due in May 1970, they achieved a rare outcome for a protest movement: complete success.

The stopping of that 1970 tour was a cathartic event: racist cricket, rugby and other sports tours from South Africa to Britain were not permitted until after the struggle to defeat apartheid was won. The African National Congress was thrilled, as were Nelson Mandela and his comrades on Robben Island, who at the time heard of the victory from furious white warders through a news blackout.

The background to that unique campaign is compellingly summarised in this booklet which also shows why protests over sports – perhaps counter-intuitively to many – played, such a critical role in the anti-apartheid struggle. After all, as South African Nobel Laureate J.M. Coetzee wrote, for white South Africans under apartheid, sport was 'the opium of the masses'.

Anyone wanting to understand the story of how, from small beginnings in the 1950s, the British Anti-Apartheid Movement eventually won this campaign should read this excellent and timely primer by Geoff Brown and Christian Høgsbjerg.

Peter Hain being removed from Oxford University v South Africa
game at Twickenham 1969

CONTENTS

INTRODUCTION

This short pamphlet aims to commemorate the fiftieth anniversary of the Stop The Seventy Tour Committee (STST) – which formed in 1969 and was the catalyst helping to generate an inspiring mass movement from below of international solidarity which included mass non-violent civil disobedience and militant direct action on a scale in the world of sport that had never been seen before in Britain. Focused mainly on the protests against the South African rugby union tour, the STST was a campaign that in defiance of police brutality and violent racist intimidation successfully halted the white South African cricket tour of England in 1970 – a famous victory over racism in general and the apartheid nature of South African sport in particular. The definitive history of the STST campaign is still to be written, and aside from a fine, inspiring work written in the campaign's immediate aftermath in 1971 by STST organiser Peter Hain, *Don't Play with Apartheid: The Background to the Stop The Seventy Tour Campaign*, and the efforts of the archivists of the Anti-Apartheid Movement (AAM), the story is too little known today – hence this pamphlet.[1]

Southern Africa – and resistance against the barbaric apartheid regime in South Africa – was one of the critical turning points of solidarity for the British (and international) Left during the long 'radical sixties', generating a strong Anti-Apartheid Movement, with parallels with the international Boycott, Divestment, and Sanctions movement (BDS) in solidarity with Palestine under Israeli occupation today. During the 1960s, black resistance and the wider anti-apartheid struggle in South Africa itself was at a low ebb in the aftermath of the Sharpeville massacre of 1960, with many leading activists in prison. In the words of Ronnie Kasrils, who would escape to London in 1965, where he recruited radical British students to undertake 'underground work' for the ANC back in South Africa (the 'London Recruits'), it was 'possibly the darkest days of apartheid, following the South African security police crackdown of 1963-66, which led to an entire liberation movement leadership being incarcerated in prison or driven into exile'.[2] With the victory of the STST, as Peter Hain once recalled, 'for the first time in ten long bitter years since Sharpeville, black South Africans and whites involved in the resistance had something to cheer about. There were people abroad prepared to risk a great deal in standing up for their rights. This was a clarion call in the wilderness, a flash of light in the dark'.[3]

In particular it traces how the question of apartheid South Africa – described by Haile Selassie at the UN in 1963 in words later made famous by Bob Marley as one of those 'ignoble and unhappy regimes that hold our brothers... in subhuman bondage' and that needed to be 'toppled and destroyed' – helped politicise and radicalise a generation of young activists in Britain.[4] Many activists were inspired by the advance of guerrilla fighters in Mozambique and Angola, and in 1967 and 1968 by the Wankie and Sipolilo campaigns, when the ANC's armed wing uMkhonto weSizwe joined fighters from ZAPU (Zimbabwe African People's Union) to fight their way through Zimbabwe into South Africa.[5] Amid the international revolutionary tumult of '1968' and workers' and student protest, these activists helped transform the movement. A limited liberal campaign based on a strategy of 'respectability' and appeals to British ideas of 'fair play' by elite figures in the world of politics, sport and civil society became a mass movement from below that inspired further anti-apartheid activism internationally and future anti-racist and anti-fascist activism in Britain.

1. A SLOW COAL TRAIN COMING: THE ROOTS OF STST

The history of racism in sport and protests and boycotts against it is a long one. There was a struggle against racist sport in South Africa before the apartheid era. But when thinking about international solidarity with non-white South Africans under apartheid in the field of sport in Britain, the high point of militancy of the STST was, with apologies to both Bob Dylan and Hugh Masekela, 'a slow coal train coming', and rested on over a decade of prior campaigning and activism.

During the 1950s, despite successes in some minor sports such as table tennis thanks to the work of the communist Ivor Montagu in expelling South Africa from the International Table Tennis Federation, when it came to major sports like rugby union, cricket and football, as Peter Hain noted in *Don't Play with Apartheid*, 'in Britain, not much attention was focused on sports apartheid until the late fifties, when Father Trevor Huddleston began to promote an awareness of South African sport through public statements and writings. Out of this increasing awareness, Campaign Against Racial Discrimination in Sport was formed in 1958'.[6]

The Campaign Against Racial Discrimination in Sport (CARDS)

CARDS was formed by figures around the Movement for Colonial Freedom (MCF), which had itself been formed in Britain in 1954. The MCF (later called Liberation) involved leading members of the Labour Party including Harold Wilson – who later became party leader and prime minister, Barbara Castle and Tony Benn. Its leading figure was the veteran socialist, campaigner and Labour MP, Fenner Brockway. He later recalled:

> South Africa represented everything to which we were opposed. Though independent it was an occupied country, a white minority denying the non-white any political rights. The distinction between its racism and the rest of the world was that, though many nations practised some discrimination, most were ashamed of it, whilst South Africa on the other hand boasted of apartheid, applauding it as the basic precept of her political philosophy... Sport was crucial because to white South Africans rugby, football and cricket are a religion. The Movement for Colonial Freedom initiated a committee against racial discrimination in sport, arranging a deputation to the High Commissioner of New Zealand, to which a rugby team from South Africa was going [in 1956]. ...[7]

The liberal objectives of CARDS were set out by its secretary Anthony Steel in 1959, who wrote of 'the contribution that the Campaign hopes to make towards the recognition by South Africa of the international principle that the only criterion for judging a sportsman is ability and keenness, and not the colour of his skin'.

The first step in establishing our Campaign was to gain the support of distinguished British people, so that it would have a considerable status. The first to lend their names as sponsors were Fenner Brockway MP, J P W Mallalieu MP (both Labour), Jo Grimond MP (Liberal), E Bullus MP (Conservative), J B Priestley, A J Ayer (Professor of Philosophy at London University), Sir Julian Huxley, the Archbishop of York, the Roman Catholic Archbishop of Liverpool, and the Chief Rabbi. We then felt able to approach leading British sportsmen with the suggestion that they sign a letter which would be sent to *The Times*, condemning the colour-bar in South African sport, as reflected at the Empire Games; and calling upon all sportsmen to work to persuade the international federations controlling each sport to adopt the Olympic principle. Twenty great sportsmen, known to millions all over the world, signed the letter published in *The Times* on 17th July 1958, two days before the start of the Empire Games.'[8]

The CARDS letter in *The Times* deplored the presence of the exclusively white South Africans at the British Empire and Commonwealth Games in Cardiff, which meant that 'the policy of apartheid should be extended even into international sport' and urged, 'athletes and sportsmen in this and other countries should take active steps through their clubs and their national associations to obtain the endorsement by their international federation of the principle of racial equality which is embodied in the Declaration of the Olympic Games'. The famous sports stars (not only sportsmen) who signed were leading footballers Walley Barnes, Danny Blanchflower, Johnny Haynes, Jimmy Hill, George Knight, Stanley Matthews and Don Revie, the motor racing champion G.E. Duke, athletes Geoff Elliott, Mike Ellis, Thelma Hopkins, Derek Ibbotson, Ken Norris and Frank Sando, the boxer Joe Erskine, the cricketers David Sheppard, M.J.K. Smith, Maurice Tremlett and Alan Wharton and tennis player Bobby Wilson.[9]

As Dennis Brutus – the poet and South African sports campaigner who would form the South African Sports Association (SASA) in late 1958 – noted in 1959:

> At the time of the Commonwealth Games at Cardiff last year, a protest was organized by Mrs Gladys Griffiths of Penarth, and more than a thousand signatories protested at the exclusion of non-Whites from the South African team ... the Movement for Colonial Freedom held a meeting in Cardiff on the eve of the Games. Through the valiant efforts of Welsh sportsmen, the matter was placed on the agenda at the meeting of the [Olympic] Federation, but London officials suppressed it in "the interests of harmony", and the absence of representatives of four-fifths of the South African population was ignored at this meeting of the "great family of nations."[10]

Anthony Steel describes the next steps of CARDS after this:

The next step was to circulate leading British Sports Clubs asking them to pass resolutions urging their national associations to raise the question of the adoption of the Olympic principle in their appropriate international federation; and in the soccer world at least, we gained considerable immediate support. Many leading clubs such as Bristol Rovers, Hull City, West Ham United, and Dundee United passed such resolutions; and indeed the Bristol Rovers resolution was signed by all the first eleven, the reserves, the chairman, manager, assistant manager, secretary, masseur, coaches and trainers! A wonderful gesture! The next objective of the Campaign was the meeting of the International Olympics Committee at Munich in May 1959. A letter instancing the flouting of the Olympic principle by South Africa and calling upon the I.O.C. to apply its own charter sincerely, was circulated amongst outstanding people all over the world ... In all, 21 great names appeared on the letter, which was sent together with a memorandum to M. Otto Mayer, the Chancellor of the Olympics Committee, who placed the matter upon the Committee's agenda. All national Olympic committees were sent copies of the letter and memorandum. At the meeting of the I.O.C, India, Egypt and the Soviet Union strongly supported the memorandum sent by the South African Sports Association and by this Campaign. To avert the possibility of expulsion, the South African official representative gave an undertaking (since confirmed by the South African

Olympic and Commonwealth Games Association—SAOCGA) that his association would do all it could to further the interests of non-white sportsmen in the Union, and would certainly have no objection to their inclusion in future South African Olympic teams, if they were good enough.[11]

One athlete – Nicholas Stacey – wrote to explain why he had joined the CARDS committee:

I recently accepted an invitation to join the Committee of the Campaign Against Race Discrimination in Sport for two reasons: As an ex-International and Olympic athlete, I know that international sport becomes a farce and mockery unless in the words of the Olympic Charter "no discrimination is permitted on grounds of race, religion or politics". If a national team is not made up of the best possible sportsmen available it ceases to be a truly national team. The aim of every aspiring sportsman is to represent his country. That some people should be denied this honour simply on grounds of their colour is as unfair as it is nonsensical. For years I ran fairly consistently second to one of the greatest sprinters in the world – Mr. Macdonald Bailey, a coloured man. Because of him I was denied almost every major athletic honour. But I would not have had it any other way. He was a better runner than I was. If we had had race discrimination in sport in England, I should have won many titles, but they would have been hollow and valueless victories. Race discrimination in sport is really a misnomer, because if there is race discrimination it ceases to be sport. In sport there should be only one criterion; that of ability. As one who believes in the Christian Faith and feebly endeavours to live out its principles, race discrimination in sport runs clean contrary to my fundamental and deeply held beliefs. I hope that the white South African national 'sporting' bodies which at the moment admit only white South Africans will immediately make their organisations truly sporting by admitting all men on equal terms. If they refuse, I believe that international sporting bodies should refuse to recognise these unrepresentative South African bodies, and that 'white-only' South African teams should be barred from international sport.[12]

So a dialectic of protest was now in play. In the face of the lobbying of elite sports officials via letters of celebrities and leading figures in the world of sport and civic society from above, and the organising of mass petitions on the grounds of a betrayal of "sporting" or "Olympic values" backed up at times with protests outside the grounds from below, representatives of white South African sport would try to promise inclusion of non-white sports players "if they were good enough". This of course was a promise never realised, given the white supremacy underpinning the policy of South African sports, one which had eerie echoes of Nazi Germany. Ritter von Halt, the Nazi sports leader, when explaining why the German Olympic team was all Aryan had said 'the reason that no Jew was selected to participate in the Games was always because of the fact that no Jew was able to qualify by his ability for the Olympic team. Heil Hitler.'[13] In fact, the link to Nazism was even more direct, as politicians who

had been members of the Afrikaner Broederbond –
apologists for Nazism – at the time of the Second
World War in South Africa (when they had been
imprisoned for sabotage and subversion), were now
in positions of power and authority in apartheid
South Africa in the highest posts of government and
their brutal security apparatus (BOSS).

Protesting the 1960
South African Cricket Tour

Soon three new factors emerged, which emboldened
the small but growing campaign in Britain. Firstly,
there was a developing movement among non-white
South Africans themselves in the field of sports
activism which now came to the fore, spearheaded by
Dennis Brutus. In October 1958 Brutus had helped
form the South African Sports Association (SASA) in
East London (in South Africa's Eastern Cape), with
the South African writer Alan Paton, author of *Cry,
the Beloved Country*, as patron, and the inaugural
conference of SASA was held in January 1959. In
October 1959, SASA successfully blocked an all-black
West Indian international team led by Frank Worrell
from touring and playing against a set of non-white
teams in South Africa. This was a controversial move
on the part of SASA, as defenders of the idea of the
Worrell tour (which included the great black West
Indian Marxist C L R James) argued that had it gone
ahead it would have allowed non-white cricketers in
South Africa such as Basil D'Oliveira the opportunity
to play against a world class international test team,
the West Indies, led by an inspiring black captain,
Frank Worrell, whose claim to captain the West Indies

team would be massively strengthened. That Dennis Brutus and SASA successfully organised to block the Worrell tour, however, laid an important new marker down about the importance of not acquiescing with anything that could be interpreted as legitimising the apartheid division of South African sport in any way.[14]

Secondly, the Indian government also spoke out against the Worrell tour, and so pressure from newly independent countries was now another new critical dimension that opened up amid the wider process of decolonisation. This force would later be harnessed by the formation of the South Africa Non-Racial Olympics Committee (SANROC) by Dennis Brutus in 1962, and strengthened further as the 1960s went on. The rise of new independent black African states and the rise of African stars in fields like athletics culminated in the formation of the Supreme Council for Sport in Africa in 1966 at the Bamako conference, shaped by Brutus and the white South African weightlifter and treasurer of SANROC Chris de Broglio. Black American athletes were also coming to the fore in the 1960s, symbolised by the courageous and inspiring stance in solidarity with the wider Black Power movement taken by Tommy Smith and John Carlos at the Mexico Olympics, and the new reality was that black American stars would boycott future Olympic Games if white South Africans were present became a new factor.[15]

Thirdly, the bloody Sharpeville massacre in the Transvaal on 21 March 1960. South African police opened fire on a crowd of thousands in the black Transvaal township while they were peacefully protesting against the oppressive pass laws. The killing of 69 people, including women and children, and injuring of around 180 others shocked millions of people worldwide and exposed for many the brutal, barbaric nature of the apartheid system.

As a result, when the white South African cricket team toured England in June-August 1960, in the immediate aftermath of the Sharpeville massacre, CARDS (which now had as its president His Grace the Archbishop of Cape Town, Professor A. J. Ayer as chairman, with Anthony Steel and Derrick Silvester from MCF serving as joint secretaries, and with its headquarters at the black civil rights activist and doctor David Pitt's surgery on 200 Gower Street in London) were pushing at an open door when they began to think about raising voices in protest. The English cricketer, the Rev David Sheppard bravely made a pioneering stand and said he would not play against the South Africans and Rev Nicholas Stacey, the former Olympic athlete, also refused to preach the 'sportsman's service' before the first test at Edgbaston.[16] CARDS did not call for people to boycott the matches, but they did organise a petition to Marylebone Cricket Club (MCC), then the governing body of English cricket.

We the undersigned regret that the South African Cricket Association did not see fit to consider for inclusion in the touring side players of non-European stock and urge the M.C.C., not to support fixture tours conducted on such a basis. We are sorry that the M.C.C. should have appeared to condone the application of the principle of Apartheid in sport.[17]

As at the British Empire and Commonwealth Games in Cardiff, there were some protests and leafletting organised outside grounds before matches, asking spectators to protest to the South African Cricket Association at its selection of a whites-only team. There was also the embryo of a more militant approach emerging amongst some activists. In Sheffield, a group of activists prepared to paint anti-apartheid slogans on the walls of the stadium one night, but the police were waiting as they arrived, arresting many of them.[18] There was some labour movement support, above all in Wales where the Welsh Council of Labour and the South Wales National Union of Mineworkers (NUM) called on Glamorgan to cancel their match.

However, the level of protest at this tour (and also at the Springboks – the South African rugby union team – tour of England in the autumn of 1960 and spring of 1961) was in general very low, certainly compared to, say, the contemporary protest marches organised by the Campaign for Nuclear Disarmament (CND) in this period. They did make a small impact, however, perhaps if only through their novelty, if nothing else. The young white South African journalist Donald Woods, for example, recalls being surprised at the protests and arguing with protesters outside Lords, defending the segregation of South African sport and questioning whether it was right to target the matches given the players were arguably not the main enemy, 'they are sportsmen not politicians'. It was only when the South African cricketer Jackie McGlew joined the ruling apartheid National Party and stood for parliament in the late 1960s after retiring from play that Woods started to question the doctrine of 'keeping politics separate from sport', which, as he put in retrospect, echoing the famous words of John Arlott – was 'a lunatic view, since sports is a part of life, and all life is connected to politics'.[19] Perhaps less as a result of the protests and more as a result of the wider feeling of public disgust among many cricket supporters after Sharpeville, the 1960 tour was the first tour of England by South Africa since 1912 to make a financial loss.[20]

The Anti-Apartheid Movement (AAM) and the 1965 South African Cricket Tour

In the early 1960s, the formation of the AAM, in which many South African exiles played a leading role, together with the fact that the liberal CARDS had failed to establish for itself any kind of activist base meant, as Brockway remembers, the Movement for Colonial Freedom 'handed over the campaign against South African sport to the Anti-Apartheid Movement'.[21] As Christabel Gurney – a AAM activist herself from 1969 – records:

Throughout the 1960s AAM supporters demonstrated at sports events involving South Africans. Cardiff and Glasgow City Councils refused to entertain a South African bowls team, there were protests against tours of South Africa by the Welsh Rugby Union and Arsenal Football Club ... At an international level the AAM worked with the South African Non-Racial Olympic

Committee (SANROC) to ensure that South Africa was excluded from the Olympic Games. It wrote to 118 national Olympic committees and [AAM secretary] Abdul Minty lobbied at the International Olympic Committee's 1963 conference in Baden-Baden. As a result South Africa was excluded from the 1964 Tokyo Olympics.[22]

Also in 1964 South Africa's ban from membership of FIFA was re-imposed successfully now the Olympics and international football had been effectively closed off to apartheid South Africa. In South Africa, the Riviona Trial saw African National Congress leader Nelson Mandela and others imprisoned for life, leading to a growing number of student protests in Britain over the question of apartheid and the radicalisation of a new generation over this issue. For example, at Oxford University, on the 12 June 1964, five hundred people, mostly students, joined a picket organised by the local AAM group with the support of the Labour Party after the then South African Ambassador, Carel de Wet, was invited to speak at Northgate Hall, the Oxford Union buildings, by the Oxford University Tories, on the very day Mandela was imprisoned. As Ian Birchall recalls 'students organised a large demonstration against the ambassador. The Oxford Union's hall was plunged into darkness when a future editor of *International Socialism Journal* [Peter Binns] removed the fuses'.[23] As Binns recalls, 'the ambassador had been invited to speak at the Union and that that was the reason why I and others thought that sabotaging the event by plunging it into darkness was the thing to do. Removing the fuses (which were in an ancient fuse box and irreplaceable) made sure that the event could not just be postponed to later in the evening but had to be abandoned altogether.'[24] Birchall then recalls:

> A "mob" – which I am proud to have been part of – surrounded the ambassador's car and let the tyres down ... The response of the University proctors was to place concern for petty regulations before justice in South Africa. A number of students (including Tariq Ali) were victimised by suspension. (One of the proctors was a Mr Bond, who was promptly labelled 'licensed to kill'.)
> These events led to the launching of a campaign for student rights, which was the first stage of a movement that was to reach culmination in 1967 and 1968.[25]

October 1964 saw the election of a Labour government under Harold Wilson, a supporter of the AAM, though nominally overseeing a British capitalist state with historic trade and military links to the apartheid South African regime. This would in time lead to a tension over approaches within the AAM, between lobbying the Labour government 'behind the scenes' and campaigning through 'respectable' protest on the one hand, and the need to still hold the Wilson government to account through grassroots pressure and direct action from below. In response to the 1965 South African rugby union tour of Ireland and Scotland, the AAM put out a public statement in April 1965 urging a boycott signed by figures including Oliver Tambo, acting president of the ANC, leading parliamentarians such as David

Ennals MP (chair of the AAM), Jeremy Thorpe MP, Lord Brockway and Eric Heffer, and the writers Basil Davidson, Ethel Mannin, Bertrand Russell and Leonard Woolf.[26]

The 1965 South African cricket tour saw the AAM organise a boycott and protests and pickets outside every tour centre. This was much wider public opposition than ever before and the most effective intervention around sport by the AAM to that point.[27] A mass petition in protest, posters stating 'Going to see the South African "Whites Only" Cricket Team? (It's Not Cricket)' and campaign badges, leaflets, stickers and balloons all circulated.[28] This had the feel of a movement getting under way, and students would play an important role – though because the cricket tour took place over the summer months, their potential ability to mobilise en masse was limited, and so it fell on the Left in various localities to organise opposition.

The AAM, in keeping with the 'respectable' nature of their protest tactics, organised to hold, launch of 'the campaign against apartheid in cricket' in the House of Commons with the legendary West Indian former cricketer and civil rights campaigner Sir Learie Constantine speaking on 23 June 1965.[29] The AAM honorary secretary, Abdul Samad Minty (who used the pseudonym S Abdul) wrote to the Queen asking her to join in the boycott, thus achieving the success of both the Queen and Prime Minister Harold Wilson staying away from any official functions with the South African team.[30] More broadly, the AAM sent 2,500 letters to 'people of some prominence, also sporting organisations, asking them to sign a declaration that they object to racialism in sport and will not themselves attend any match in which the South African team is playing'. They heard back from figures including Benjamin Britten, many MPs, the Rev David Sheppard, actors, musicians and the Welsh Basketball Association among others. 'To help swell the protest we wrote to the C[onstituency]. Labour Parties, Liberal Parties, West Indian organisations in the areas, CND groups, Committee of 100, and various other organisations who have in the past expressed an interest in this movement or are affiliated to us. These include church organisations.'[31]

Pickets and protests ranging from 20 to 200 strong, were held outside various grounds during the tour, and trade unionists and Labour Party activists often came to the fore in helping co-ordinate them In Derby, for example, Tom Pendry, then a young trade unionist with the NUPE union (now UNISON), helped co-ordinate a 100-strong picket line at Queen's Park in Chesterfield with the local Derbyshire branch of the NUM when the South Africans played Derbyshire on 28 June 1965. 'The line not only had miners, with Dennis Skinner at the fore, but other workers in the area, as well as Anti-Apartheid supporters from Derbyshire and Yorkshire', Pendry recalls. Ethel de Keyser then invited Pendry to speak the next day at a national AAM rally in London's Trafalgar Square alongside national figures such as Nobel Peace Prize winner Philip Noel Baker MP, the Bishop of Johannesburg, David Ennals MP, the actor Patrick Wymark, liberal leader Jeremy Thorpe and leading South African communist Ruth First. 'My part in the rally was small but well received, as it demonstrated that sport-loving people were prepared to forego their natural desire to attend a favoured sport in the interest of a greater ideal – namely, the conquering of racism in sport, and we would do so wherever racism reared its ugly head'. But Pendry recalls Ruth First's 'eloquence and passion, saying that South Africa was isolating itself from the world':

"You must pass from verbal condemnation to practical action", she urged. "The people of Britain must see that their government stops dragging its feet at the United Nations whenever the question of South Africa comes up. The guilty men of apartheid are not only those who make the laws in South Africa, they are among us here in Britain – those who draw the profits from apartheid".[32]

As with David Sheppard before, one cricketer in 1965 honourably publicly refused to play the white South Africans, Stanley Jayasinghe, from Sri Lanka. 'I'm a bit of a rebel', he told *Anti-Apartheid News*, 'I decided five years ago I'd never play the SA team again' after his experiences in 1960, when 'afterwards, at the socials, they were standoffish with a lot of us chaps from the Commonwealth. I'd been boycotting South African goods even before that, but decided this wasn't enough'. 'You can call it childish but I think of millions of dark fellows in South Africa who get no chance to exercise their rights, who carry passbooks around like dogs wearing a collar, of the torture in the jails, and I used my freedom to express my disapproval of the whole SA system. I know I'm one of the lucky ones, coming over here and having all doors open for me, that's why I'm particularly concerned about all those for whom this is impossible in South Africa.'[33]

As well as a higher level of public protest, another new dynamic began to emerge in the mid-1960s as the local black community in Britain started to organise against apartheid. In November 1966, a 'West Indian Committee Against Apartheid' led by W. Wilkie organised a protest about the 'Rest of the World' against Barbados match set for March 1967 as the 'Rest of the World' included a Rhodesian player and two white South Africans in its team. On their leaflets, they highlighted a quote from Sir Learie Constantine, 'Must we be hosts to people whose guests we can never be?'[34] Rising black British protest amid the growth of 'Black Power' would play an increasingly important role in the Anti-Apartheid Movement, linking the struggle against racism in South Africa with the need to fight racism and break the 'colour bar' of institutional racism closer to home.

The 'Spirit of 1968' and the turn towards direct action

The year 1968 was famously marked by a series of protests and demonstrations in Britain, with students at their heart, whether the Hornsey art college occupation or the growing anti-Vietnam War demonstrations, including the march on the US embassy in Grosvenor Square in March 1968 which saw violent clashes with the police. Some of the earliest student protests that year in Britain took place over the question of solidarity with apartheid

South Africa, and in their new militant tactics, epitomised the wider revolutionary 'spirit of 1968'.

In January 1968, the white-only University of the Orange Free State rugby union team, known as the Shimlas, arrived from South Africa in Britain for a tour. Originally scheduled to play ten different university rugby teams, by the time they arrived, campaigning by student unions and anti-apartheid students at institutions such as Durham, Sheffield, Bristol, London, Sussex and Exeter – in part on the grounds that the tour was a propaganda event funded by the South African External Affairs Department – meant most of these matches were cancelled and only three games were still lined up to play.[35] The first of these was scheduled to take place on 31 January 1968 against Newcastle University at Gosforth. Fifty students from Newcastle and Durham led by one young student with a megaphone organised a protest with placards, but about fifty police placed on duty ensured they were kept away from the game itself unless they discarded their placards. Frustrated by not being able to prevent the match from going ahead, students bought tickets and entered the ground. During the match Ian Taylor, a member of the International Socialists (IS) and a Durham student said to his fellow Durham student IS member Anna Paczuska, 'It will be no more than a ten pound fine to run on the pitch and stop this. Are you up for it?' Yes, came the answer. 'Good. Pass it along'. Five minutes later, thirty student protesters, including several black students, then did something up to that point unheard of – they rushed onto the pitch – and again twice more during the game as well.[36] They made the national TV news. The *Daily Telegraph* reported 'the semi-comic atmosphere of siege' in which the game was played, and that 'the incident provided the crowd with some light relief as young men and girls in jeans and miniskirts played a game of "catch me if you can" with burly, heavy-coated policemen'. 'In the second half a girl dressed in green tights and jumper with a snappy red waistcoat ran onto the pitch and, almost playfully, invited half a dozen young policemen to catch her. She led them a merry dance until she tripped and then was transported bodily to the sidelines. The crowd watched it all with good humour'.[37] There were no arrests. About thirty protesters were escorted out of the ground by police, and one publication reported how 'fifty policemen stood by while the demonstrators chanted "apartheid is nasty" and paraded with banners saying "for pity's sake stop it" and "we must oppose".'[38]

The second game the Shimlas were set to play was up at the University of St Andrews in Scotland on Friday 2 February 1968, despite the public opposition of David Steel, the Liberal MP and AAM President and the university rector-elect, Sir Learie Constantine, who wrote a telegram to St Andrews students: 'Fixture with South Africans deplorable. Government which by legislation reduces human beings to lower animals unworthy associate with decent governments and people. Statement that our attitude brings politics into sport highfalutin nonsense. South African government began by taking away discretion sporting bodies by legislation'.[39] Encouraged by Constantine, once again about 100 student protesters from across Scotland and the North of England, with banners declaring the match was 'a disgrace' to 'human rights' and slogans including 'we say no to apartheid every time', 'the rugby club does not represent us', 'Anti-Apartheid' and 'this match is deplorable'. The Durham University student paper, the *Palatinate* reported how after the second scrum, which was the signal agreed on beforehand, fifty student protesters ran onto the pitch, occupied it and so halted play, supported by scores of St Andrews students in their red gowns on the touchline (St Andrews University students had been threatened with severe disciplinary action if they invaded the pitch themselves). After the pitch invasion, the Vice-Principal Professor Norman Gash, a Tory historian, strode onto the pitch and requested the students to leave: 'I fancy you are not members of this university. You are guests. I would like you to behave as guests. You have made your demonstration and will you now please go? I don't want to have to bring in the police'. *Palatinate* reported how 'the professors voice was drowned in shouts of refusal'. Gash threatened the protesters with police dogs. Protesters jeered, asking how the dogs would know the difference between protesters and players. Gash called for the police and left the pitch. At this point, a section of the wider rugby-supporting crowd (including a racist element who called the protestors 'nigger lovers', a sign of a wider racist backlash which would receive a huge boost with Enoch Powell's 'Rivers of Blood' speech two months later) began shouting 'off' 'off' at the protesters. Declaring 'let us rush them off the pitch', this element proceeded to link arms and charge the protesters. While many demonstrators were violently cleared from the field in this manner (with one Durham female protester assaulted in the process), a minority of the protesters managed to re-assemble again in the middle of the pitch, disrupting the game for twenty-five minutes in total before the police arrived and began to make arrests.[40] Even after the match finally re-started, individual protesters tried to interrupt play at various times by running onto the pitch, but they were ignored by the players, who even knocked one such protester to the ground. Twelve students in total were arrested from a range of universities, including Durham, Newcastle, Edinburgh and Dundee, and were held for four hours, charged with trespass and breaching the peace under Scottish law. Funds were raised to pay for their fines, though it seems all charges were eventually dropped.[41] In the aftermath of these two disrupted matches, both of which achieved a high level of media attention due to the new tactics of direct action, the third match set to be held in Lancaster was abandoned – so overall a clear victory to the protesters.

If David Sheppard was right to describe cricket's relationship to apartheid and racism as the biggest challenge to face cricket in its history, this relationship was now in the national spotlight as a result of the controversy around the South African 'Cape Coloured' player Basil D'Oliveira. D'Oliveira had been unable to further his career under apartheid and so moved to England, and in 1966 was selected to play in the Test side for England against the West Indies. In September 1968, D'Oliveira was refused permission to enter South Africa with the MCC team as part of a tour, with Prime Minister John Vorster declaring that with D'Oliveira in the side 'it is not the MCC team – it's the team of the Anti-Apartheid Movement'.[42] This incident, which led to the cancellation of the MCC tour, had echoes of the case of Kumar Shri Duleepsinhji, a brilliant South Asian-born batsman who played for Sussex country cricket club and who was selected for England in 1929. One of *Wisden's* five 'cricketers of the year' that year, he played in the first Test match against the touring white South African side. When South Africa complained about his presence, he was quietly dropped from the England side for the rest of the series. Prime Minister Harold Wilson condemned the decision, stating: 'Once the South Africans had said that they were not taking a player we wanted to send, I would have rather thought that put them beyond the pale of civilized cricket'.[43] Yet in December 1968, the MCC voted 4,664 to 1,214 to continue hosting tours from South Africa, even if there was still no meaningful progress being made towards non-racial cricket in the country.[44] With another tour from South Africa now looking very likely in the summer of 1970, the Anti-Apartheid Movement once again, in 1969, began collecting signatures for a petition against such a tour taking place. By mid-July 1969, some 2,000 signatures had been collected, but already there was a growing mood among many younger activists that more effective and militant action than simply petitioning and protesting was now needed.[45] Peter Hain, a student whose family had been forced into exile from apartheid South Africa and who was a leading member on the radical wing of the Young Liberals (the youth group of the Liberal Party), and other students, mostly around the Young Liberals and AAM networks, had led disruptive pitch invasions against the white South African Wilf Isaacs Invitation cricketing XI in July 1969, and also protests at the tennis Davis Cup between Britain and South Africa in Bristol.[46] Christabel Gurney remembers the protest against the Wilf Isaacs XI as one of the first anti-apartheid activities I was involved in ... the people I remember sitting on the Oval pitch with were Wilfred Brutus (Dennis's brother) and Isaiah ... an older South African – they were from SANROC and I met them through the AAM'.[47] In a press release issued during these Wilf Isaacs protests, Hain wrote that 'our protest will take the form of a non-violent token disruption. Its aim will be to demonstrate the seriousness of our intention to massively disrupt the 1970 tour, and at the same time to give the MCC an opportunity to call off the tour. We regard the tour of the white South African team to Britain as an outright capitulation to racialism and an affront to Britain's coloured community. And we will do all in our power to ensure that this tour is a failure, should it take place.'[48] Their sense that there was now the need for a formal organisation to co-ordinate such militant direct action would culminate in September 1969 with the formation of a new group, the Stop The Seventy Tour Committee, with one aim – to stop the cricket tour in the next summer of 1970 and by any means necessary.

2. THE STOP THE SEVENTY TOUR CAMPAIGN

After discussion, Dennis Brutus from SANROC, Peter Hain, a national executive member of the Young Liberals, and Hugh Geach, secretary of the Reading Joint Anti-Apartheid Committee, agreed the name, easily shortened to the snappy acronym 'STST', and wrote to fifty organisations inviting them to join. A few days later the *Guardian* published a letter from Hain pointing out:

> The consequences of another refusal by MCC to cancel the tour should not be underestimated. The token disruptions during the recent tour of the Wilf Isaac XI to Britain and the Davis Cup match at Bristol demonstrated the seriousness of threats to massively disrupt the 1970 tour.[49]

STST's public launch came at a press conference in the White Swan, a Fleet Street pub, on 10 September 1969. Supporting organisations included the Anti-

Apartheid Movement (AAM), the radical Christian organisation CHURCH, the International Socialists (IS, which in 1977 became the Socialist Workers' Party), the Movement for Colonial Freedom (renamed Liberation in 1970), the National Union of Students, the Reading Joint Anti-Apartheid Committee, SANROC, the United Nations Student Association, the Young Communist League (the youth wing of the Communist Party of Great Britain) and the Young Liberal Movement.[50]

The Springboks rugby union tour

As the focus was on stopping the South African 1970 cricket tour, the STST committee 'only became interested in Rugby as a second thought'.[51] At this point, the only fixture being targeted in the forthcoming South African Springboks rugby tour was the international against England at Twickenham in December.

For the South African government, rugby union could never be a second thought. It was *de facto* the national game. John Vorster, the South African Prime Minister, spoke at the official farewell function for the team the night before they left for England.[52] There were tensions between the STST and many in the AAM leadership, who wanted to keep the movement under their banner. Direct action didn't sit easily with some of AAM's more staid members (though of course many younger members were actively involved) nor with its lobbying, working as a pressure group for example, getting 103 MPs to sign an AAM letter of protest to the MCC.[53] There was also the possibility it could trigger legal action, and the AAM feared it would be charged with conspiracy and closed down. Dealing with these contradictory pressures, Ethel de Keyser, AAM executive secretary, explained how the strategy was 'to raise anti-apartheid feeling to such a pitch that the tour will become a financial flop with people staying away and the cost of maintaining police protection'. This didn't mean doing nothing at the matches. On the contrary:

We plan to continue holding demonstrations at the matches, although we do not aim to disrupt them. We aim to stop them. We would like no games to take place ... we're not involved in running onto pitches, pouring on gravel, that sort of thing. I'm not saying we *disapprove* of people doing this, but we are not doing this ourselves.[54]

In the event, AAM and STST worked together to build a mass movement, which mushroomed to the extent that by one estimate, 50,000 people demonstrated, around 200,000 leaflets were produced and distributed and, at its height, there were some 400 local action groups.[55] The famous propaganda poster of police brutality in the Cato Manor township outside Durban produced by the AAM was hugely popular, 'if you could see their national sport you might be less keen to see their cricket'.

The STST Committee formed a loose leadership, quickly establishing contacts around the country. As Dennis Brutus put it 'our strategy was based on letting the local people choose their own strategy. We never told them what to do. We just said, the "Springboks will be here next, do what you have to do."'[56] Ernest Rodker was a veteran of the Committee of 100, the non-violent direct action group opposed to nuclear weapons. At its peak in 1961 it brought thousands of protesters to Whitehall with hundreds being arrested. Ernest got involved with STST, and later in an interview recalled:

If you could see their national sport, you might be less keen to see their cricket.

Anti-Apartheid Movement, 89 Charlotte Street, London W1.

I think something happens, you know, a spark, it's the right tune. The student movement was blossoming and there were various activities going on in the student movement. The students were terribly important because the rugby tour was going to university towns and playing university teams ... And so the students were very involved in coming out and demonstrating against the matches. So it just coalesced *really*. The groundwork had been done.[57]

Anna Davin, a student at Warwick University at the time, remembered:

Much of the action was also independently organised and carried out. Students from many universities would travel to the Springboks, matches and join the protests, often with no direct contact with Hain's group ... They were very organised, making sure they wore the right clothes to minimise getting caught or hurt, and they would "keep an eye on each other to make sure no-one got left behind or lost.[58]

'Don't Scrum with a Racist Bum!'

As the Springbok team arrived for their twenty-five match tour, on 30 October 1969, the Reading Anti-Apartheid group was waiting for them with banners, shouting 'Don't Scrum with a Racist Bum!'. 'No to 'Boks' was painted in large letters in prominent spots on the team's route into London.[59] After an evening reception at the South African embassy on Trafalgar Square, they found themselves unable to leave. In an 'undignified huddle' in the embassy foyer, looking 'sheepish', they had to listen to demonstrators shouting 'Go home Springboks', until the police escorted them to their coach.[60] The first match was against Oxford University on 5 November 1969, a high profile game due to be shown on TV. A 'Fireworks Day Committee' was set up to organise the demonstration. Dennis Brutus had travelled to Oxford few weeks earlier to meet the local student anti-apartheid committee. He found them in a pub,

> ...smoking pipes and drinking sherry. And I said, "Hey, what are you guys going to do? This is terrible. I've come here for a meeting and there's nothing happening". I think I made them feel bad enough. So I went back to London and told everyone, "There's going to be national television, but no protest, nothing."[61]

Two weeks before the match, 'Oxford Rejects Apartheid', a slogan painted with weed killer, appeared on the pitch in letters five foot high. John Sheldon, former Joint General Secretary of PCS (Public and Civil Service Union), then a student at Ruskin College, was on the Fireworks Day

Committee, and he later recalled how the sporting angle meant that anti-apartheid as a campaign found deep wells of support in the British working class:

> I'm very interested in Rugby League, which is a working class sport. And it was the fact that [in 1957] the South Africans refused entry to someone called Billy Boston, who played on the wing for Wigan, a very famous rugby league player, a black Welshman, and I think that that was the first illustration that I had about what apartheid must mean. So I think that brought it home to me. Billy Boston was a hero to many millions of people in the north of England. For him not to be able to go to South Africa, I think fetched that home to lots of ordinary people, if you like, the guy on the street, that perhaps this was something which was affecting them as well as just affecting some people in far off South Africa – we're talking about 30 odd years ago. So there was lots of things that drew the anti-apartheid cause towards British trade unionism that just maybe Vietnam did not do.

The Fireworks Day Committee organised large numbers of supporters ready to occupy the pitch to get tickets. John Sheldon and Mac Reid, another committee member, having been pulled in for an interview by a number of senior police officers, the university club officials called off the match, 'because of the risk of violence.'[62] After tortuous negotiations, the match was switched at the last minute to Twickenham, 'the home of English rugby'. Though it had a capacity of 60,000, there were just 6,000 spectators watching the match accompanied by a thousand demonstrators chanting and 'sieg heiling' throughout – and managing to very briefly disrupt the match through pitch invasions.[63] Outside the ground a loudspeaker van led the demonstration, 'All-whites must get off the rugby field. We don't want the cancer of racialism here.'[64]

That day's *Guardian* carried an interview with John Taylor, the Welsh and British Lions player who had seen the reality of apartheid on the 1968 Lions tour, announcing he was no longer willing to play against the Springboks, 'the first prominent figure to break through the facade of solidarity the rugby authorities have been so desperately been trying to build'.[65]

The violence of the State unleashed

By now the STST was front page news and the campaign took off. The *Guardian* asked 'Have the Springboks already lost?' noting that, while the next match against Midlands Counties East at Leicester on 8 November had a pitch easier to defend, there was 'a strong radical element at Leicester University who will not easily be deterred (Leicester was the first university to hold a successful sit-in)'.[66] This radicalism was seen in the militant slogans of the protesters and the multiracial nature of the crowd: 'Racialism, out, out, out, ... Apartheid, out, out, out, ... Black and white unite and fight', 'Class war in, race war out', while a group of Black Panthers and Leicester University students led the march with a banner 'Smash Racialism'.[67] A thousand police confronted three thousand demonstrators – all but a hundred outside the ground laying siege to it, repeatedly trying to burst through police lines. 'Policemen's helmets rolled in the streets and demonstrators' banners ripped and splintered... There were one or two really tough skirmishes ... and some National Front members ... joined in the scuffles and got the worst of matters.'[68] A group from Nottingham including some electrical engineering students managed to smuggle insulated bolt cutters into the ground and cut the power lines, briefly shutting down the floodlights.[69] A few of the hundred protestors inside got briefly onto the pitch.

Afterwards the local chief constable claimed 'Today you have seen all that is best in the British copper ... I think everybody was quite happy with the outcome. The demonstrators demonstrated and the game was played'.[70] In reality, one young eighteen year old student protester at the time, Lindsey German (later convenor of the Stop the War Coalition), who was attending her first protest (after not being allowed to attend the Vietnam War marches the previous year by her mother) remembers most of all 'the incredible violence of the police against the protesters to protect the match'.[71] As even the *Sunday Telegraph* reported put it:

> In a scene of the utmost confusion policemen, demonstrators and Saturday afternoon shoppers could be seen leaning against the walls in pain or doubled up on the road, writhing in agony. One young constable was doubled up in pain after a heavy kick in the groin. Suddenly a flurry of policemen burst from the side of the road. They

scattered the demonstrators, pushing many of them face down in the road. Two reporters of the *Sunday Telegraph* were held in the air and thrown against a brick wall, suffering cut arms and slight cuts to the face. Shaken housewives returned to their homes in side streets near the ground weeping. Some lost half their shopping under thousands of thudding boots. Many spent 20 minutes struggling through police and demonstrators to reach refuge.[72]

A police sergeant and 21 demonstrators were taken to hospital. The STST committee received 38 documented complaints. John Sturrock, Leicester University Students Union secretary, said there would be 'a do or die' attempt to halt the match planned at Manchester. 'People are in a very ugly mood now.'[73] The strength of the Leicester protest saw the question raised:

If 500 policemen are needed to keep 500 demonstrators (gathered at 12 hours notice) behind a fence 150 yards long for an hour and a half, how many policemen are needed to keep 2,000 demonstrators (given 6 months notice) behind the boundary of Lord's cricket pitch for 5 days?[74]

The next three matches in South Wales (against Newport, Swansea and Gwent) in November 1969 presented a new challenge, as here rugby was almost a working-class religion. The small peaceful protest at the final Gwent match reflected something of this. Led by members of Gwent Socialist Charter, and supported by South Wales miners, a hundred and fifty protestors, women in black sashes, men in black armbands, leafleted spectators, then stood in silent protest at the entrances to the Ebbw Vale Welfare Sports Ground and finally, from their vantage point on the hillside road, 'their chants of "Springboks out" welled into the ground in the bottom of the valley'.[75] Around 700 protested in Newport, and then even larger numbers joined the protest at Swansea on 15 November, where, boosted by a recent successful sit-in, backed by their union, students had set up a Town Committee. Its public meetings in the run up to the match grew and so did the police's interest. A week before the match a student stumbled on plainclothes officers going through student records in the university registry.[76] The 2,000 strong demonstration on the day itself was militant, chanting 'Paint 'em black and send 'em back', 'Jack in the 'Boks', and 'Swansea Shame'.[77] Yet as Richard Jones and Tony Goodchild recalled in 2004, it quickly turned into a police riot:

As the demonstration reached the St Helen's rugby ground, the first snatch squads were sent in to arrest organisers. One of the protesters recalls, "I was wrestled to the ground and given a good kicking. My glasses were ripped off my face, and I spent most of the rest of the day wandering around in a fog, but my comrades held on and dragged me back to safety." In spite of their efforts, the police failed to make a single arrest at this stage. This appeared to drive them into a frenzy, and it was the less militant demonstrators, unprepared for what was to come, who bore the brunt of an attack that shocked all who witnessed it. Kath Eilbeck, a local student teacher, witnessed the police directing ambulances through the crowd in an effort to break it up: "The ambulances were empty, and when they got clear they just turned round and came back again." Inside the ground some 70 demonstrators made it onto the pitch and stopped the match for 20 minutes. They paid for their courage with the most vicious attacks imaginable. Dragged off the pitch by police and specially hired vigilantes, they were then thrown to other "stewards" who had been allowed by the police to arm themselves in preparation. Television news showed one student being held over the railings and mercilessly clubbed as the men in blue looked on laughing. One indication of the ferocity of these attacks is the fact that 200 demonstrators were treated for injuries. The battle outside the ground went on throughout the match, lasting some two hours. There were large numbers of arrests, mostly on trumped-up charges. Among the local workers arrested were steel workers, electricians, engineers, miners, teachers, lecturers, a play leader and a public relations officer.[78]

Twenty protesters were so badly hurt by police and stewards they had to be taken to hospital, including five who were knocked unconscious.[79] As one protester, Fred Fitton recalls,

It was my first term in Swansea Art college. At this time I did not really understand what a union was and I had never been on a demo before. In Cambridge I had seen people come back from Red Lion Square with flags but I understood very little. I went along with others out of curiosity. The demo was against the Springboks tour and

I remember students coming in buses from all
over the UK ... When I got to the flag pole in front
of the guildhall I remember seeing for the first
time the International Socialists ... holding flags
were Tony Goodchild of the University and Brian
Rees who later worked at the DVLA. Tony told
me recently that they called the demo. Also there
were people from the Labour Party and Ian Bone's
group from the Swansea Anarchists. Howell Bithel
from Brynmill Labour would have been there
because he led Anti-Apartheid in Swansea for
years after that.

This was the most violent demo that I have ever
been on and since that time I have worked on
three miners strikes, 74' and '84. I saw terrible
violence at Grunwicks and Wapping but on this
demo the fighting just appeared to go on for a
long while. The police were throwing students
out of the Rugby ground as if they were a scrum
all rolling around in a ball and I think it was
because they thought they had full support of the
rugby crowd. Yet these people who supported the
police that day would have met the same violence
outside the pits only a couple of years later. Yes I
saw anarchists throwing bricks but only at police
vehicles. The police did not appear to care what
they did and I am amazed that no one was killed
that day.

The Swansea Left from then to now has been
made up of many who cut their teeth that autumn
day in Swansea. In Swansea it normally rains but
it did not that day. What I do remember is that
when it came to the court cases, and there were

mania it was a complete shambles because one copper would claim he arrested a student inside the ground and another had made the claim that he arrested the same student outside the ground. As a result I think many were let off. Two years later I was teaching in St Joseph's Catholic school in Port Talbot and I took some of the older students on an anti-apartheid demo in London shouting "Free Nelson Mandela". This was at the time when our papers called him a terrorist.[80]

The day after Swansea, Hain issued a STST statement 'demanding a full public enquiry into the Swansea demonstration and particularly into the role played by the rugby vigilantes. This private army of rugby thugs was responsible for some of the most systematic and brutal mob violence ever seen on peaceful demonstrators in Britain'.[81] The response of the Labour Home Secretary James Callaghan, who as a backbencher, had been the first ever parliamentary advisor to the Police Federation, was to call a conference of chief constables. Callaghan told parliament:

These developments are placing a very heavy responsibility on the police service. I have, therefore, decided to call a conference of chief constables in those areas where games are still to be played in order to discuss the best way in which the responsibilities of the police can be carried out. Among the questions that I shall ask to be examined is the extent to which stewards are helpful. At two previous games, there was little or no complaint of the activities of stewards, but it is clear that their behaviour at Swansea caused a great deal of public disquiet.[82]

Callaghan told police chiefs that stewards were to be barred from dealing with demonstrators, but he refused to concede that the police were to blame for the violence at Swansea.

We are also getting the usual job lot of anarchists – people who are not interested in supporting a cause but in causing disruption. One can be sure that, if you get a group of anarchists attached to a procession, whatever the leaders of the procession have agreed with the police, the anarchists will not carry it out. I am very concerned to see that the police are not made the butt of mischief makers and those seeking violence.[83]

The mass anti-Vietnam War demonstration outside the US embassy in Grosvenor Square had caught the British police on the hop. Running to catch up, they now made sure that they were fully informed about the STST through infiltrating the groups. Special Branch produced regular secret reports giving details on how many coaches were coming to the next match, who had booked them, and so on.[84] Hain recalls how police planted evidence on STST activists, from drugs, knives, and broken bottles.[85] Special Branch agents infiltrating left-wing campaigns were nicknamed 'hairies'. One called 'Mike' was 'virtually Hain's second-in-command'.

Special Branch had targeted the campaign after warnings that there was likely to be 'blood on the streets'. Mike has since died but his handler, Wilf, is still very much alive. "I don't think Hain ever realised he had a hairy as his number two." Mike provided the intelligence that enabled the police to deal with the disruption planned for a big rugby game between the Springboks and the Barbarians at Twickenham. The demonstrators planned to throw smoke bombs and metal tacks onto the pitch, but thanks to Mike the police were ready with sand and electric magnets. News film of the time clearly shows them being used. There was the inevitable inquest into how the plan had been thwarted. 'Hain felt, quite rightly, that there was a spy in their midst,' says Wilf. 'Mike looked down the room at one poor devil and said: 'I think it's him!' He was thrown out and Mike survived.[86]

The movement reaches its height

Yet police intimidation and repression couldn't stop the growing momentum of the movement, and at the Springboks match against London Counties at Twickenham on 22 November, the STST recorded what Hain recalls as 'the most effective direct-action protest so far', as well over 2,000 protesters got inside the ground, some wearing Springbok rosettes, some having cut their hair and shaved their beards. A hundred protesters got through the police cordon onto the pitch, and one seizing a corner flag managed to plant it in the middle of the field. Play was stopped for ten minutes and again briefly a couple more times, despite the fact the police cordon was now some 800 strong, and despite brutal violence against protesters from police and racist rugby fans (including some members of the fascist National Front). Another 1,000 demonstrators who had not made it into the ground then marched on the police station to demand the release of a dozen demonstrators held inside.[87]

In late November, the National Union of Students (NUS) – then under the (broadly) left-wing leadership of Jack Straw – resolved to support the STST campaign at its conference 'in the form of a unanimous vote in favour of a comprehensive motion on the subject'.[88] The NUS conference gave a boost to the turnout at the Manchester demonstration on 26 November a few days later. University and college students' unions mobilised across the North and Midlands. Three hundred students attended a lunchtime meeting in Liverpool University with Peter Hain and African National Congress member Aziz Pahad. The day before the Manchester demo, six Black Panthers marched into Manchester cathedral, stopping a service for racial harmony. They declared their support for the demonstration but insisted that people recognise that racism exists not only in South Africa but in Manchester as well. On the day, 7,000 protesters, including members of the Institute of Science and Technology UMIST Rugby Club, 150 priests and members of the university Conservative Association, assembled at the university. Nearly 2,000 police were on duty for 'the biggest demonstration they had ever had to deal with.'[89] Janet Whelan, a junior clerk in the probation service and a member of Manchester Anti-Apartheid, remembers 'feeling so encouraged at the start of the march, by the sheer numbers present'.[90] Six students were at the front carrying a black coffin. Painted with the words 'Remember Sharpeville', it contained tools for breaking through the back gate to the stadium. Engineers, scaffolders, draughtsmen and members of the Manchester and Salford Trades Council carried their union banners. The mile-long march stopped a couple of hundred yards from the stadium expecting to follow the route agreed with the police.

At this point the front sector of the march was standing peaceably facing down Talbot Road (i.e. the way they should have been) and waiting for the rest of the marchers to join up. Then, without any warning, the police attacked the front of the march. A wedge of police drove in from the right about 20 yards from the front rank, attacking individual marchers and smashing the black and white coffin which had been the march figurehead.[91]

The march was broken up. As police horses now moved in, the *Daily Telegraph* saw how:

Demonstrators threw shoes, clothing, placards and even themselves at the horses but without effect.... The mob fell back and tried to push into Boyer Road, another way to the main gate, but they were checked by more police. Marchers attacked police who tried to remove struggling, screaming troublemakers.[92]

One hundred and fifty demonstrators were arrested, more than 40 inside the ground, and 77 were charged. In the Chief Constable's view 'the vast majority of the student demonstrators were "very nice young people" and their own official leaders had done their best to control them. There was, however, a "militant lunatic fringe" which as usual tried to join in.[93] The Student Union organised legal support, listed 28 complaints and voted to pay

£100, the maximum allowed, to help with fines.[94] With scores of complaints the Chief Constable was forced to organise an inquiry.[95]

As Hain recalled, 'in the three weeks that followed the Swansea match, the campaign reached its height in terms of impact and effect. The collective result of the Swansea violence, the Twickenham disruption, the massive force of the Manchester demonstration and the next match at Aberdeen was to put the tour in serious jeopardy', not least as Aberdeen on 2 December – where 1,000 marched in the city to the stadium chanting 'Wilson out, Powell out, racialism out' – would see 'the most successful disruption of the campaign' with a pitch invasion by about 100 demonstrators.[96] As Brutus recalls,

> The students started a fight among themselves. The cops ran there to stop it. And while the cops were there, students invaded the pitch from the other end. Then they all ran into the centre of the field and piled on top of each other. There was this huge mound of bodies. And then, by agreement, everybody clutched everybody else. So when the cops dragged out a body, they got about six bodies attached to it. Best of all, while this was happening, guys climbed the goal posts and stood on the crossbars and gave the Nazi salute – a marvellous photograph for the press.[97]

The police made 98 arrests, including 29 women, almost all students. One of those arrested remembers 'we all got a night in the cells (and had a ball!, filling them completely. Others arrested after us were bussed down to the beach and dumped so they had to walk back, arriving after the game's end. We in the cells were charged with breach of the peace, and later were each fined £15'.[98] While those arrested planned various fundraising activities to help pay the substantial fines, one of their number, Audrey Farrell – a member of Aberdeen International Socialists – had the audacity to suggest inviting John Lennon to play at a benefit gig. Lennon couldn't come, apologising for being a little busy, but he sent a cheque for £1,500 to pay all the fines, so further boosting the campaign.[99]

Four days later, on 6 December, 2,000 marched to Murrayfield and the Scotland international match in Edinburgh. As secretary of the Dundee University Socialist Society, Europe Singh had organised coaches to the demo. In front of a 30,000 crowd, a dozen jumped the barrier, Europe and Paul Holborow grabbed the corner flag running towards the centre of the pitch before being stopped. Jeannie Robinson and Europe were carried off the pitch. His turban and shoes torn off, Europe remembers being 'lifted aloft over fences by a phalanx of police several rows deep.'[100] Every one of the 26 arrested complained of police brutality.[101] Manchester engineers – the District Confed committee – wrote to the Home Office asking for a meeting about police behaviour at Springbok matches.[102]

Two thousand marched in Cardiff on 13 December, where the match was played behind a ten foot high barbed wire fence which made it look like an internment camp.[103] The next massive mobilisation by the STST was set to take place on 20 December at Twickenham, when the Springboks played their international game against England,

and by now the relentless protests and mass media attention had forced the South African Cricket Association so make a statement claiming that its team due to come to Britain the following summer would be selected on a non-racial basis. As the well-known cricket commentator John Arlott wrote, 'It must now seem that the demonstrators, by their action against the Springbok rugby tour, have in a few months achieved more than the cricket officials have done in 15 years of polite acquiescence.'[104]

Match day did not start well for the Springboks as they left their hotel for Twickenham. Some of them had already lost sleep as Ernest Rodker had booked himself into their hotel, identified three or four of the players' rooms and then called fellow STST activist Mike Craft to glue the door locks.[105] Then, as South African rugby vice-captain Tommy Bedford recalled, he:

> ...was sitting on the coach with some of his
> team-mates when a guy got in the driver's seat.
> He looked like a driver because he had a cap on.
> He started the ignition and pulled away from the
> hotel in London's Park Lane. And then all hell
> broke loose. The police outriders had been caught
> by surprise. Half the team weren't even on the
> bus. And where on earth were they going? As they
> sped past Green Park underground station one of
> the players managed to get his hands round the
> driver's neck. The bus crashed into half a dozen
> cars. The police arrived. Chaos. The guy had tried
> to hijack the Springbok rugby team. And all this
> only four hours before kick-off.[106]

Outside the ground, a 5,000 strong demonstration

organised by the AAM was led by peers, bishops, MPs and public figures. Afterwards, folksinger Julie Felix sang to the demonstrators.[107] Inside the ground, two Young Liberals, Mike Findley and Peter Twyman had spent a few hours practicing handcuffing themselves to a pole in the middle of a lawn. Together with Ernest Rodker and a friend they were sitting in special seats.

> We were in the front row of the pitch. We [Rodker and friend] would be a diversion and then [Findley and Twyman] would run up to the goalposts and lock themselves ... onto the goalposts... [T]he place was swarming with police. We were surrounded by pro-rugby supporters ... we got onto the pitch and immediately we were stopped and we sat down and they started to drag us.[108]

Rodker's diversion worked:

> We got all the attention and then this other person got to the goal posts and then locked on... the police were obviously well prepared and they had bolt-cutters and it didn't last long. But it got quite a lot of publicity and it would have been seen by 80,000 people.[109]

British Fascists were now actively supporting the Springboks. Paul Foot reported a National Front circular calling on members to come to the England-South Africa game at Twickenham.

> This occasion... will provide us with our most important propaganda opportunity of the winter period. We intend to counteract the fraudulent posturing of the left by turning up in strength and displaying a number of big banners. Through the

generosity of Mr Chesterton our tickets for the event will be heavily subsidised and maybe free for some members.[110]

Jim Nichol, an IS member, remembers the match as scary as 'we found ourselves in the same section as the NF. There was one almighty fight with fists flying. There were dozens involved'.[111] Bob Newland, a YCL member, pulled out his placard in the crowd, his protest lasting just seconds before he was pounced on by police.[112] Newland would in 1971 become one of the 'London Recruits', smuggling in ANC leaflets to be exploded out of litter bins in South African cities. He remembers a number of the 'London Recruits' in 1969-70 'went into bars and saw tins on the bar labelled 'Give Hain Pain', collecting money to take action against him'.[113]

Yet it was clear the STST's campaign was having a major impact – the flag of the ANC even briefly flew over the Springboks' London hotel at one point thanks to an intrepid STST activist.[114] Further mass protests followed in the new year, including at the International games in Dublin, Cardiff and at Twickenham. As Peter Hain recalls,

Wherever the team went, resting, training or playing, it was under siege. Over Christmas, two months into the tour, the players took a step inconceivable in the annals of Springbok history and voted to go home. But the management, under political pressure, ordered them to stay. The tour finally staggered to an end with the players bitter and unsettled. For the vice-captain, Bedford, it proved a cathartic experience. Within a year he publicly stated I [Peter Hain] should be listened to, not vilified, and praised our objectives. Although his response was a relatively isolated one in South Africa, it signalled the huge and destabilizing impact of our campaign. For the first time, the Springboks, accustomed to being lionised, perhaps the leading national rugby team in the world, had instead being treated as pariahs.[115]

Ireland

The largest single protest during the STST campaign – indeed what Hain calls 'the biggest and best demonstration of the whole tour' came in Dublin early in the new year in 1970 when the Springboks arrived to play their International match against Ireland in January 1970.[116] Another match scheduled for 29 November 1969, the match against Ulster, had been the only fixture to be cancelled on the grounds of security – but even in November there had already been opposition to the Springboks' tour shown by the Northern Ireland Civil Rights Association and a one thousand strong students meeting at Queen's University, Belfast.[117] The first protest against the Springboks coming to play Ireland in Dublin in the New Year was less well known for its militancy, the Catholic university of Maynooth with a hundred-strong 'all clerics' protest. Less surprisingly, the Irish Rugby Football Union's headquarters had slogans painted on it, its secretary had his home picketed, as were the Irish national teams trial matches. The goal posts at University College Dublin rugby ground were sawn down, 'a protest against the continued use of the pitch by the Irish team and club members selling tickets for the match.' There were no photographers on the runway as they came off the plane otherwise the loaders would refuse to handle the flight.[118] Sixty demonstrators sat down in the road at the airport then the team's hotel.

As nowhere else on the tour, trade unions took a lead, no doubt encouraged by the Irish Anti-Apartheid Movement, founded by Kader and Louise Asmal in 1963, and which organised daily meetings and one all-night vigil outside the Springbok's hotel. The Dublin Council of Trades Unions held a large public meeting and set up an action committee. The Irish Transport and General Workers Union called on people to join the protests and promised to support any members disciplined by their employer for taking part. The Post Office union tried to withdraw phone and mail services to the hotel. There was an argument in the press whether journalists should be able to refuse to report the match by not crossing the picket line. The president of the republic, Eamon de Valera, decided not to accept an invitation to the match and the Taoiseach, the prime minister, decided not to receive the team. No member of the government attended.

People's Democracy in the North called for its supporters to join the protest:

We have too much apartheid here between the two communities to encourage any more racialists... There are already too many political prisoners in Ulster for us to welcome emissaries of a government that ... interns without trial even

more political prisoners than the Mad Major (James Chichester Clark, prime minister of Northern Ireland) and his associates.[119]
The struggle for civil rights continues. It is a worldwide movement. To allow the Springbok team to Ireland and without our protests is to insult our black brothers in South Africa – with whom we have a lot in common.[120]

While they helped publicise the campaign, unions' calls for action were largely unsuccessful. The Aer Lingus staff voted not to block the flight bringing the team to Dublin. Attempts to block the team hotel's phones did not come off. The day before the match, Catholic and Church of Ireland clerical and divinity students carried out a 24-hour vigilant fast in central Dublin protesting the team's selection as 'a complete negation of the teaching of Jesus.' On the day up to 10,000 marched to the ground at Lansdowne Road – the largest demonstration in the city in half a century, led by prominent Irish public figures including the writer Conor Cruise O'Brien, the former rugby international A.R. Foster and the newly elected Westminster MP Bernadette Devlin, who came with a contingent from the North organised by People's Democracy. Inside the ground the pitch was barricaded with barbed wire.[121] After the match, the team entered a city hotel for dinner, through a phalanx of police to chants of 'Paint them black and send them back' and under a hail of eggs, bottles and stones. A few minutes later demonstrators were baton charged by the police. Protests continued at the hotel and the British Embassy until late into the night.[122]

Getting the 1970 cricket tour stopped

By Spring 1970, the STST had not just evolved into a mass movement but one with a sense of growing momentum that was prepared to go all out to stop the 1970 cricket tour. One STST Executive member, Mike Craft, who had been involved in the Campaign for Nuclear Disarmament (CND) said the enthusiasm for the anti-apartheid cause during the Springbok rugby protests had been greater than CND at its height.[123] Though it had a 'Special Action Group' for necessarily secretive actions by a minority, it had also a formal organisation and on 7 March 1970, a national STST conference was held with 300 delegates and speakers including the South African-born sociologist John Rex, Jeff Crawford of the newly formed West Indian Campaign Against Apartheid in Cricket and the cricket player Mike Brearley, who had seconded a vote of no-confidence in the MCC committee in December 1968 that had been proposed by David Sheppard.[124] Brearley had visited South Africa to play on the MCC tour of 1964, and he has recalled how 'exposure to the system of apartheid' was 'an education for me, firming up my belief that it was wrong to play sport against a country where discrimination governed all areas of life, including sport'.[125] Critically for an organisation based on civil disobedience, STST recognised the importance of winning mass support among workers and had a STST trade union organiser, Bryan Thomas, and STST secured the support of 20 trade unions. For the first time a largely student-driven movement had managed to pull significant trade union support.[126] This was central to getting the TUC in April 1970 to back the call for the invite to the South African cricket team to be withdrawn.[127] This was a real achievement. As Jack Jones, General Secretary of the Transport and General Workers Union, 1968-78, later vice president of the Anti-Apartheid Movement, pointed out in an interview about his visit to South Africa in 1973:

> ...I tend to link the attitudes of a lot of leaders in the TUC and the trade unions to their attitudes towards race and colour because of racial discrimination. They dragged their feet on that for many years. The idea of getting legislation against discrimination was opposed by people like Victor Feather and on the political side by Bob Mellish, very strongly, and, equally, their attitude towards opposition to apartheid, or even anything very much to do with South Africa, was lukewarm. The older tradition of respectability continued such as the Fair Cricket Campaign with two Conservative MPs among its members. The former England cricket captain David Sheppard, Bishop of Woolwich continued to campaign against apartheid in sport while refusing to support direct action.[128]

Though the STST prioritised direct action, it always looked outwards and attempted to build alliances with other organisations where possible, and its partnership with the AAM was particularly important. As Christabel Gurney, a leading AAM activist has recalled:

> The demonstrations against the rugby Springboks were remarkable in a number of ways. They

involved a wide range of organisations taking a lead in different places, under the dual umbrella of the AAM and STST. They combined mass protest with direct action. They maintained their momentum for over three months – from 30 October [1969] to 2 February [1970]– and covered 22 venues all over Britain, from Exeter in south-west England to Aberdeen in north-east Scotland, and in Ireland. The AAM sent posters and altogether 200,00 leaflets to local anti-apartheid groups and sympathetic organisations in every town where a match was scheduled... Altogether it has been estimated that more than 50,00 people took part in protests against the tour.[129]

Marylebone Cricket Club (MCC), which had issued the invitation to white South African cricket to tour in 1970, was always a bastion of conservatism, Lord Monckton once remarked, 'I have been a member of the Committee of the MCC and of a Conservative Cabinet, and by comparison with the cricketers, the Tories seemed like a bunch of Commies'.[130] But now it was a besieged bastion as a result of the STST campaign. Letters to the MCC from its members urging it to stand firm give a sense of the atmosphere of crisis of the time. One labelled the STST a 'complete negation of all this country stands for' and felt the MCC were defending 'the last bastion of what remains of the British way of life'. Peter Hain was seen as a 'dangerous anarchist and communist', and it was noted that if the STST can 'smash this tour they will turn to other things'. Another described the

STST campaign as 'persistent mob pressure and an attempt at neo-communist rule'.[131] Representatives of county clubs were often landed gentry, and as one secretary said of them on 14 December 1969, 'this was their opportunity to apply all their dislike and loathing of permissiveness, demonstrators and long hair. Staging matches is their chance to make a stand against these things'.[132]

For Stuart Hall and his co-authors of *Policing the Crisis* (1978), the STST 'exhibited all the concentrated force of a single-issue campaign, limited in scope, but wide enough to involve young liberal people... very considerable numbers of young people, sensitised by the events of 1968, were recruited into the politics of the demonstration by the clarity of its anti-apartheid appeal'. The STST represented 'the transmission of the spark of student politics to a wider constituency and field of contestation – the "politics of the street"', or in this case – the politics of the cricket and rugby grounds, which, as Hain recalled, by the end of the tour 'were looking more like armed camps than peaceful playing fields'.[133] As a United Nations report commented in retrospect, 'Virtually every match was played in an atmosphere of siege. Large numbers of police had to be summoned to protect the grounds, and rows of policemen encircled the playing fields to prevent demonstrators from invading them. Barbed-wire fences were erected inside and outside the grounds, and police dogs were brought in and held in reserve at strategic points.'[134]

On 19 January 1970, STST activists and others co-ordinated raids on 14 of 17 county cricket grounds, daubing them with slogans, digging up a small part of Glamorgan's Cardiff ground and spraying weed killer on Warwickshire's Birmingham ground, creating mass media publicity and a clear warning of what activists would do with respect to direct action should the 1970 cricket tour go ahead.[135] Another factor was the deepening anger among Britain's black community at apartheid, as evidenced by the formation of the West Indian Campaign Against Apartheid in Cricket by Jeff Crawford, a member of the West Indies Standing Committee. On 3 February 1970, Frank Cousins, chair of the Community Relations Commission said in a letter to the Home Secretary the tour would do 'untold damage to community relations'.[136] The West Indian Campaign Against Apartheid in Cricket discussed a one day strike on London transport by black West Indian workers to coincide with first match at Lord's.[137] As Elizabeth Williams has noted in her work on black British solidarity with the anti-apartheid struggle, Ethel de Keyser argued that black British pressure 'tipped the balance at Lords' in favour of the protesters among officials.[138] Finally, growing, wider international pressure in the arena of international sport amid decolonisation so brilliantly mobilised by Brutus and SANROC was also increasingly making itself felt. In March 1970, the general assembly of the Supreme Council for Sport in Africa met – and this led to a coordinated boycott threat of the upcoming Commonwealth Games by many independent African states.[139]

Hitting racism for six – victory and legacy

By May 1970, the growing campaign and pressure meant that the possibility of a demonstration of tens of thousands outside Lord's for the first planned match in the South African cricket tour of 1970s, indeed perhaps a demonstration of 100,000, was now a credible one.[140] With the first big demonstration outside Lord's already built for, on 20 May 1970 Home Secretary James Callaghan had the Cricket Council in his office to tell them to reverse their recent decision to go ahead with the tour. Few organisations outside the racist Conservative Monday Club were still publicly supporting it. Indeed, even the delegates at the Police Federation conference cheered the news that the Home Secretary had asked the cricket authorities to cancel the tour.[141] On 22 May 1970, the Cricket Council announced the tour was off. *The Times* reported the response from some of the leading campaigners to their victory:

> Mr. Peter Hain, chairman of the Stop the Seventy Tour Committee, said it was extremely courageous of the Government in acting to pull the situation out of an entrenched position. "I would hope the Conservative Party will come out in support of the Labour Party in these circumstances." He described it not as a backing down for British cricket but an advance to a situation where racialism would be rejected in international sport. Mr. Dennis Brutus, president of the South African Non-Racial Open Committee for the Olympic Games, said: "The way is open to real progress towards non-racial cricket in South Africa."

Mr. Jeff Crawford, secretary of the West Indian Standing Conference, commented: "I would hope that the momentum we have gained for the fight against racialism will go on in Britain." The Bishop of Woolwich the Right Rev. David Sheppard, Mr. Reginald Prentice and Sir Edward Boyle, of the Fair Cricket Campaign, said: "This wise decision is a victory for reason. It is not a surrender to intimidation or blackmail. By its decision the Cricket Council has committed itself firmly to the principle of non-racial cricket in the future."[142]

Hitting the tour finances was never going to work. The South African government would ensure tours were not stopped by lack of money. But while rugby supporters always outnumbered the protesters by a large margin, their numbers fell. Some fans began to question whether their 'religion' could exclude players because of their race. For all the boost that racism received from Powell's 'Rivers of Blood' speech, the anti-immigration laws in 1968 (and later on in 1971 and 1981, the rise of the National Front, Thatcher's notorious fear of being swamped, interview on TV and so on), the campaign against apartheid grew. As Christabel Gurney puts it,

The AAM built on the groundswell of opposition to sports apartheid to build mass campaigns against the many other ways in which Britain supported apartheid. In June 1970 the newly elected Conservative government lifted Labour's partial arms embargo. Buoyed by the success of the Springbok campaign, the AAM rallied a wide coalition of trade unions, churches, students and community organisations to oppose arm sales.

The TUC Congress pledged to back workers who refused to work on arms for South Africa, and in the event only four Wasp helicopters were supplied. In the 1970s the focus shifted to British companies which invested in South Africa and direct action became part of the range of tactics employed by the wider movement. Prominent among these companies was Barclays Bank. Starting in 1971 activists attended its AGMs in an attempt to stop it approving its annual accounts. Students were in the forefront of the campaign to make Barclays pull out of South Africa, with action ranging from Essex students setting fire to a Barclays branch to student unions banning Barclays from having stands at Freshers Fairs. As anti-apartheid campaigning became mainstream in the 1980s, the memory of the 1969–70 Springbok campaign remained as an inspiration, Britain's first significant anti-apartheid victory.[143]

Moreover, as Peter Hain later wrote of the STST, 'the most important factor in its development and amazing depth of support and commitment was that it gave expression to a deep and almost enraged opposition to racialism amongst many people in Britain'.[144] Hain himself would go on to form the short-lived Action Committee Against Racialism and then help found the Anti Nazi League in 1977, which played a critical role in confronting and defeating the rising threat of the fascist National Front. The STST protests – which proved to be a model for the Australian Campaign Against Racialism in Sport (CARIS), which alongside activists in New Zealand the organised mass protests against the Springboks rugby union tour of 1971 and successfully stopped the 1971 cricket tour of Australia – made an impact directly on South African sportsmen who now came to understand the full reality of the apartheid situation once isolated. South African fast bowler Peter Pollock, a week after the cancellation of the 1970 tour, for example, said 'Sports isolation now stares South Africa in the face, and to creep back into the laager is no answer. Sportsmen who genuinely feel there should be multi-racial sport should say so'.[145] Graeme Pollock – a brilliant South African batsman – later recalled how he felt when the 1968 tour by England to South Africa was called off as Vorster wouldn't allow Basil D'Oliveira to play as it would make England a 'team of the Anti-Apartheid Movement':

> I was 24. We didn't give too much thought to the people who weren't given the opportunities. In hindsight we certainly could have done a lot more in trying to get change in Southern Africa. I was still a young guy. We'd had a good series against Australia in'67 and we probably at that stage had our best side ever. Mike Procter, Barry Richards, Eddie Barlow, my brother Peter – there were really classy cricketers. Poor old Barry played just four Tests, Mike Procter seven. But at the same time Peter Hain and his guys got it absolutely right that the way to bring about change in South Africa was through the sport. It was difficult for 22 years and lots of careers were affected, but in hindsight it was needed and I'm delighted it did achieve change in South Africa.[146]

In 1977, isolation meant the South African minister

for sport, Piet Koornhof had finally been forced to admit that 'play and sport are strong enough to cause political and economic relations to flourish or collapse'.[147] In 1995, FW de Klerk, the last South African head of state during the apartheid era, was asked by Tom Pendry, at the time the British Shadow Minister for Sport, 'what was the most compelling reason for abandoning apartheid?' 'He replied that the trade boycotts were relatively easy to overcome, but that his country was a sport-loving one. The people yearned for a return to international competitions that they had been denied entry to.'[148]

Perhaps the most critical impact of the protests was made among those on the front line of fighting apartheid in South Africa itself. As Tennyson Makiwane of the ANC told a meeting of Surrey AAM activists in London in December 1969, Africans rejoiced at seeing the 'White supermen' of the Springbok rugby team ridiculed by the protests.[149] As Jonathan Steele wrote in the *Guardian* on 5 March 1970:

It is not hard to find South Africans who are delighted by the demonstrations against the Springboks. Go into Soweto, or any other township, and just start talking to people. When they hear an English accent, and if you are not accompanied by a white South African, the masks fall. Eagerly, they want the news confirmed: "Is it true that they are having to use a thousand police to hold back the demonstrators today? Is there really that much feeling against South Africa?" ... Their views on the Springbok tour were straightforward. They were against it. And so were their neighbours, and anyone else you talked to.[150]

The protests gave a huge morale boost to prisoners of the apartheid regime. The white liberal Hugh Lewin, imprisoned for years in Pretoria for his activism in the African Resistance Movement, had a news blackout, but the fact his warders were huge rugby supporters meant he heard them starting to swear about the 'betogers' – demonstrators – and moaning about 'that bastard Peter Hain'. Lewin detected in the quality of his soup on Saturday evening how successful the protests had been that day – the poorer the soup, the more successful the protest.[151] Moses Garoeb, a leading freedom fighter in the South West African Peoples Organisation (SWAPO), later told Peter Hain that STST had been an inspiration to SWAPO cadres in the African bush as they heard the news on their radios. Hain replied that 'it was the dedication and sacrifices of people like them which inspired us to campaign even more vigorously'.[152]

We might also recall the words of Tommy Bedford, the Springbok vice-captain, who was in the eye of the storm created by the STST:

> We spent all our time surrounded by police cordons and barbed wire, never mind having our bus hijacked (on the morning they played England at Twickenham), and then in Dublin, being confronted by demonstrators lying in the street to stop us getting to Lansdowne Road.[153]

Yet as Bedford put it:

> Nineteen sixty-nine was a watershed in many ways. It was the beginning of the end. But despite everything since, including the World Cup triumph [1995], we still haven't managed to get

the black-white mix right. Not just in rugby but in all sports. And I don't know how long it will take until we do.[154]

The struggle against racism in sport, and in wider society, continues. In terms of the Springboks at least, when they triumphed in the rugby World Cup in Johannesburg in 1995 (a moment commemorated in film by Clint Eastwood's 2009 *Invictus*), there was just one black player, Chester Williams, in the starting XV. By the time of their second World Cup win in 2007, there were still only two players. In 2019, in Yokohama, seven black players ran out in its starting side – including the captain Siya Kolisi and two players, Makazole Mapimpi and Cheslin Kolbe, who would score the crucial tries to make sure of the win over England in the final. As Kolisi put it in the aftermath of their victory, 'We come from different backgrounds, different races and we came together for one goal ... I have never seen South Africa like this. We were playing for the people back home. We can achieve anything if we work together as one.'[155] For Ronnie Kasrils, 'the Springboks' glorious Rugby World Cup victory has its springboard in those game-changing Stop the Racist Tours of anti-apartheid protest of yesteryear. Now with a black African as captain of an inspirational team the clarion call to eject racism from all sport and wider society is deafening!' [156]

Robert Archer and Antoine Bouillon, *The South African game: sport and racism* (London: Zed Press, 1984),

Douglas Booth, *The Race Game: Sport and Politics in South Africa* (London: Frank Cass, 1998).

Roger Fieldhouse, *Anti-Apartheid: A History of the Movement in Britain; A Study in Pressure Group Politics* (London: Merlin Press, 2005).

Peter Hain, *Don't Play with Apartheid: The Background to the Stop the Seventy Tour Campaign* (London George Allen and Unwin, 1971).

Peter Hain, *Outside In* (London Biteback, 2012).

Peter Hain, 'Militant Action Against Sports Apartheid', in Michael Lavalette (ed.), *Capitalism and Sport: Politics, Protest, People and Play* (London Bookmarks, 2013).

Peter Hain and Andre Odendaal, *Pitch Battles: Protest, Play and Prejudice* (London Rowman & Littlefield, May 2020),

Ken Keable (ed.) *London Recruits: The Secret War against Apartheid* (Pontypool: The Merlin Press, 2012).

Peter Oborne, *Basil D'Oliveira: Cricket and Conspiracy* (London: Time Warner, 2005).

Lee Sustar and Aisha Karim (eds.) *Poetry and Protest: A Dennis Brutus Reader* (Chicago: Haymarket, 2006).

Elizabeth M. Williams, *The Politics of Race in Britain and South Africa: Black British Solidarity and the Anti-Apartheid Struggle* (London B Taurus, 2017).

List of matches of the 1969–70 South Africa rugby union tour of Britain and Ireland with estimated approximate size of protest mounted

Versus

Oxford University, 5 November 1969, Twickenham, London – 1,000 protesters inside the ground

Midland Counties East, 8 November 1969, Welford Road, Leicester – 3,000 protesters outside ground, 100 inside

Newport, 12 November 1969, Rodney Parade, Newport – 700 protesters outside ground

Swansea, 15 November 1969 St Helens, Swansea – 2,000 protesters outside, at least 100 inside

Gwent, 19 November 1969, Ebbw Vale – 150 protesters outside

London Counties, 22 November 1969, Twickenham, London – over 2,000 protesters inside, 1,000 outside

North West Counties, 26 November 1969, White City Stadium, Manchester – 7,000 protesters outside

Ulster, 29 November 1969, Ravenhill, Belfast – match called off

New Brighton and North of Ireland, 30 November 1969, New Brighton – unknown

The North, 2 December 1969, Aberdeen – 1,000 outside, 100 inside

Scotland (Test match), 6 December 1969, Murrayfield, Edinburgh – 2,000 outside, hundreds inside

Aberavon/Neath, 10 December 1969, Talbot Athletic Ground, Aberavon – small protest outside

Cardiff, 13 December 1969, Cardiff Arms Park, Cardiff – 2,000 protesters outside

Combined Services, 16 December 1969, Aldershot Military Stadium, Aldershot – small protest outside

England (Test match), 20 December 1969, Twickenham, London – 5,000 protesters outside

South West Counties, 27 December 1969, Exeter – 500 protesters outside

Western Counties, 31 December 1969, Bristol – 500 protesters outside

North East Counties, 3 January 1970, Gosforth – 1,000 demonstrate outside

Midland Counties West, 6 January 1970, Coventry – up to 1,500 demonstrate outside

Ireland (Test match), 10 January 1970, Lansdowne Road, Dublin – up to 10,000 protesters outside

Munster, 14 January 1970, Limerick – up to 500 protesters outside

South of Scotland, 17 January 1970, Galashiels – small protest outside the ground

Llanelli, 20 January 1970, Stradey Park, Llanelli – small protest outside the ground

Wales (Test match), 24 January 1970, Cardiff Arms Park, Cardiff – up to 5000 protesters outside

Southern Counties, 28 January 1970, Gloucester – large demonstration outside the ground

Barbarians, 31 January 1970, Twickenham, London – up to 6,000 protesters outside, 500 inside

Geoff Brown, student activist in 1968, Anti Nazi League organiser, union tutor and activist, now writing a history ‹from below› of the long 1970s in the Manchester area, currently focusing on anti-racism. His publications include 'Pakistan: Failing State or Neoliberalism in Crisis?', *International Socialism*, 150, (2016), 'From Below: a handbook for career-makers in FE' in *The Principal: Power and Professionalism in FE*, eds. Maire Daley, Kevin Orr and Joel Petrie (IoE Press, 2017) and 'John Tocher and the limits of commitment', *North West Labour History*, 42, (2017).

Peter Hain, now Lord Hain of Neath, grew up in apartheid South Africa until his parents were forced into exile in 1966. A leading member of the Stop The Seventy Tour campaign, the Anti-Apartheid Movement and the Anti-Nazi League, he served as Labour MP for Neath between 1991 and 2015 and was a senior minister for 12 years in Tony Blair and Gordon Brown's governments. He is the author and editor of over twenty books, including *Mandela: His Essential Life* (Rowman & Littlefield, 2018) and (with Andre Odendaal) his co-written history of the anti-apartheid sports struggle, *Pitch Battles: Protest, Play and Prejudice* (London, Rowman & Littlefield, May 2020).

Christian Høgsbjerg is a Lecturer in Critical History and Politics in the School of Humanities at the University of Brighton. Among other works, he is the author of *C.L.R. James in Imperial Britain* (Duke University Press, 2014) and co-editor (with David Featherstone, Chris Gair and Andrew Smith) of *Marxism, Colonialism and Cricket: C.L.R. James's Beyond a Boundary* (Duke University Press, 2018). He is a member of the editorial board of *International Socialism*.

1   Peter Hain, *Don't Play with Apartheid: The Background to the Stop the Seventy Tour Campaign* (London, George Allen and Unwin, 1971) and the Anti-Apartheid Movement Archives at the Weston Library, University of Oxford (afterwards listed as AAM), many documents from which are digitalised online at https://www.aamarchives.org/.

2   Ronnie Kasrils, 'Introduction', to Ken Keable (ed.), *London Recruits: The Secret War against Apartheid* (Pontypool, Merlin Press, 2012), p.1.

3   Peter Hain, *Sing the Beloved Country: The Struggle for the New South Africa* (Pluto, 1996), p. 61.

4   Bob Marley, 'War' (from *Rastaman Vibration*, 1976). The lyrics are almost entirely derived from a speech made by Ethiopian Emperor Haile Selassie I before the United Nations General Assembly on 4 October 1963.

5   Many thanks to Christabel Gurney for this point.

6   Hain, *Don't Play with Apartheid*, p. 106.

7   Brockway, Fenner, *Towards Tomorrow: The Autobiography of Fenner Brockway* (London, Hart-Davis, MacGibbon, 1977), p. 212.

8   Anthony Steel, 'Sports Leads the Way' *Africa South*, Vol. 4 No. 1 (Oct-Dec 1959), pp. 114-115

9   'Race Discrimination in Athletics', *The Times*, 17 July 1958.

10   Dennis Brutus, 'Sports Test for South Africa', *Africa South* Vol. 3 No. 4 (Jul-Sept 1959), pp 35-39. Gladys Griffiths had graduated in French from Somerville College, Oxford, and was a teacher in Newport at the time of her marriage. Throughout her life, with the full support of her husband, she was a tireless campaigner for social rights and justice. She corresponded regularly with Professor Dennis Brutus, the South African poet and scholar who was imprisoned in 1963 for eighteen months on Robben Island in the same prison as Nelson Mandela. After his release from prison, Dennis Brutus always stayed in the home of D.R. and Gladys Griffiths on his visits to Wales. https://biography.wales/article/s6-GRIF-ROB-1915. On the protests, according to Christabel Gurney the 'Socialist Medical Association (I think) was involved in this and it was supported by the South Wales Miners Federation (again, the CPGB were strong in the miners' union).' Christabel Gurney, personal correspondence with Christian Høgsbjerg, 23 June 2019.

11   Anthony Steel, 'Sports Leads the Way' *Africa South*, Vol. 4 No. 1 (Oct-Dec 1959), pp. 114-11.

12   Nicholas Stacey, 'The One Criterion', *Africa South*, Vol. 4 No. 1 (Oct-Dec 1959), p. 116.

13   Hain, *Don't Play with Apartheid*, p. 45. In fact, at the 1936 Berlin Olympics, as Tony Collins helpfully pointed out to us, 'the Nazis allowed the German-Jewish fencer Helene Mayer to compete (she won a silver) as a PR whitewashing exercise to help the IOC's claim that the games were "non-political".'

14   See Lee Sustar and Aisha Karim (eds.) *Poetry and Protest: A Dennis Brutus Reader* (Haymarket, 2006), pp. 129-130.

15   Hain, *Don't Play with Apartheid*, pp. 98-100. Sustar and Karim (eds.) *Poetry and Protest*, pp. 133-134.

16   Jon Gemmel, *The Politics of South African Sport* (Routledge, 2004), p. 120.

17   Leaflet handed out by AAM and CARDS during 1960 tour, AAM 2227, digitalised at https://www.aamarchives.org/archive/campaigns/sport/sp001-south-african-cricket-tour-1960.html.

18   See the short piece in the 'Memories' section of the AAM website by Andrew Burchardt about action against the Springbok game in Sheffield in 1960, https://www.aamarchives.org/archive/campaigns/sport/mem04-andrew-burchardt.html

19   Mihir Bose, *The Spirit of the Game: How Sport Made the Modern World* (Hachette, 2012), p. 325. Donald Woods would famously befriend black activist Steve Biko.

20   Gemmel, *The Politics of South African Sport*, p. 120.

21   Brockway, *Towards Tomorrow*, p. 212.

22   Christabel Gurney, 'In the heart of the beast: The British Anti-Apartheid Movement, 1959–1994' in *The Road to Democracy in South Africa, Volume 3, International Solidarity* (South African Democracy Education Trust, Unisa Press, 2008). Our thanks to Christabel for sharing this essay with us. SANROC moved its headquarters to London in 1964 South Africa was finally expelled from the Olympic movement in 1970. See also AAM 1439 – a letter from Abdul Minty to Richard Thompson 10 March 1964, stating 'the campaign against race discrimination in sport has disbanded here and our movement has done most of the work in this field. I visited Baden Baden when Dennis [Brutus] could not attend and we were very pleased with the decision of the Olympic Committee'.

23   Ian Birchall, 'Oxford Mandela Demo 1964', online at http://grimand-dim.org/historical-writings/19952007-oxford-mandela-demo-1964/

24   Peter Binns, personal communication with Christian Høgsbjerg, 23 September 2019.

25   Birchall, 'Oxford Mandela Demo 1964'. See also Tariq Ali, *Street Fighting Years: An Autobiography of the Sixties* (London, Verso, 2018), pp. 102-103.

26   AAM Press Release, 3 April 1965, AAM 1433.

27   This said, the sense in which South Africa's 1965 tour of England essentially passed off without a hitch comes through strongly in an official video made about the tour available on Youtube, 'Springbok 65 - South Africa's tour of England | Cricket History' https://www.youtube.com/watch?v=t3T8KASh8hM

28   On the popularity of AAM badges (like CND ones) with the young, see correspondence of the AAM with Henry F Orpens in April 1965, AAM 1439. For a copy of the AAM poster 'It's Not Cricket' produced for the 1965 tour, see https://www.aamarchives.org/archive/campaigns/sport/po193-'it's-not-cricket',-1965.html

29   See AAM press release, dated 12 June 1965. AAM 1439.

30   See letter from S Abdul to Sir Douglas-Home, President of the MCC,

31   'Cricket' [AAM internal report on the 1965 protests], AAM 1439.

32   Tom Pendry, *Taking It On the Chin: Memoirs of a Parliamentary Bruiser* (Biteback Publishing, 2016), pp. 248-250.

33   AAM 1439.

34   See leaflet in AAM 1429 / AAM 1439.

35   *Natal Witness*, 28 November 1967. See also *Palatinate*, 30 November 1967. Cuttings here (and in publications listed below with respect to these protests) in AAM 1433 and courtesy of the private collection of Anne Paczuska.

36   *Northern Echo* 1 February 1968, which includes a photo of Ian Taylor being carried off by police, and information from Anna Paczuska, 15 September 2019. See also the photo in *The Times* 1 February 1968. For an obituary by Jock Young of Ian Taylor (1944-2001), see *Guardian*, 24 January 2001, online https://www.theguardian.com/news/2001/jan/24/guardianobituaries2

37   *Daily Telegraph*, 1 February 1968.

38   *The Journal*, 1 February 1968. The *Guardian*, 1 February 1968.

39   'Sir Learie condemns match', *AIEN*, 31 January 1968.

40   *Palatinate*, 8 February 1968; *The Courier and Advertiser*, 3 February 1968.

41   *The Courier and Advertiser*, 3 February 1968.

42   Hain, *Don't Play with Apartheid*, pp. 78, 82. On D'Olivera, see also Michael Brearley, *On Cricket* (London: Constable, 2019), pp. 119-134. For a good overview of the whole controversy, see Peter Oborne, *Basil D'Oliveira: Cricket and Conspiracy* (London, Time Warner Books, 2005).

43   Quoted in Douglas Booth, 'Hitting Apartheid for Six? The Politics of the South African Sports Boycott', *Journal of Contemporary History*, 38, 3 (2003), p. 480.

44   *Britain and Apartheid Sport: Breaking the Links* (Anti-Apartheid Movement, June 1983), p. 2.

45   S Abdul to chair of International Cricket Conference, Lords, 11 June 1969, AAM 1439.

46   Hain like some other radical Young Liberals saw himself as a 'libertarian socialist' by this time as a result of the radicalisation of 1968. See Peter Hain, *Outside In* (London, Biteback Publishing, 2012), p. 46.

47   Christabel Gurney, personal information, 7 October 2019.

48   Young Liberals News Press release, 5 July 1969, AAM 1439.

49   'Tours by South African Sportsmen', *Guardian*, 22 August 1969, p. 8

50   Hain, *Don't Play with Apartheid*, p. 121.

51   'Have Springboks already lost?' *Guardian*, 27 October 1969, p1.

52   'Tour teams given pledge by Vorster', *The Times,* 29 October 1969

53   Roger Fieldhouse, *Anti-Apartheid: A History of the Movement in Britain* (London: The Merlin Press, 2004), p.97.

54   'Who's behind the Springbok demos', *Sunday Telegraph*, 9 November 1969, p19. Emphasis in the original.

55   Hain, *Don't Play with Apartheid*, p. 196.

56   Sustar and Karim (eds.) *Poetry and Protest,* p. 135.

57   Interview with Ernest Rodker (2013), AAM Archive, Bodleian Library, online at https://www.aamarchives.org/file-view/file/7831-int21t-ernest-rodker.html

58   Reminiscences of Anna Davin (20 April 1984), in Caroline Hoefferle , *British Student Activism in the Long Sixties* (Routledge, 2013), p140.

59   Hain, *Don't Play with Apartheid*, p. 128.

60   Wallace Reyburn, *There was also some rugby*, (Stanley Paul, 1970) p12. The players were to spend much of the next three months on hotel rooms watching TV which at the time was banned in South Africa.

61   Sustar and Karim (eds.) *Poetry and Protest*, p. 136.

62   Interview with John Sheldon by Christabel Gurney (2000), AAM Archive, Bodleian Library, online at www.aamarchives.org/interviews/john-sheldon.html; 'Springbok protests "will be peaceful"', *Guardian*, 29 October 1969.

63   Hain, *Don't Play with Apartheid*, p. 131. See also *Morning Star*, 6 November 1969, and the Pathé film, 'Springbok demonstration (1969)' online at https://www.youtube.com/watch?v=MvqNVb0cIPE

64   *Leicester Mercury*, 5 November 1969, p. 1.

65   'Lion forward refuses - to play Springboks', *Guardian*, 5 November 1969, p. 1. See also Tony Collins, *A Social History of English Rugby Union* (Routledge, 2009), p. 180.

66   'Have Springboks already lost?, *Guardian*, 27 October 1969.

67   *Morning Star*, 10 November 1969. See also 'Recalling the Welford Road rugby match which caused a storm of protest 50 years ago', *Leicestershire Live*, 6 August 2019, https://www.leicestermercury.co.uk/news/history/recalling-rugby-match-caused-storm-3174056

68   *Leicester Mercury*, 8 November 1969 p1.

69   Pete Loewenstein, interview with Geoff Brown, 23 September 2019.

70   'Battle fails to stop the Springbok match. Police rescind "go gently" order', *Sunday Telegraph*, 9 November 1969.

71   Interview with Lindsey German by Christian Høgsbjerg, 20 June 2019.

72   'Battle fails to stop the Springbok match', *Sunday Telegraph*, 9 November 1969.

73   'More say: Stop tour', *Guardian*, 17 November 1969, p.1.

74   Peter Thompson, 'Looking Ahead', letter to *The Times*, 10 November 1969, p. 9.

75   'Ulster may not play S. African', *Guardian*, 20 November 1969. Hain, *Don't Play with Apartheid*, p. 133.

76   Richard Jones and Tony Goodchild, 'When Swansea mauled

racism', *Socialist Worker*, 9 October 2004, https://socialistworker.co.uk/art/2675/When+Swansea++mauled+racism+ , accessed 03/09/2019. On the Newport protest, see *Morning Star*, 13 November 1969.

77   *Socialist Worker*, 20 November 1969.

78   Ibid.

79   Collins, *A Social History of English Rugby Union*, p. 179. See also *Socialist Worker*, 20 November 1969.

80   Fred Fitton communication to Geoff Brown, 10 August 2019.

81   Hain, *Don't Play with Apartheid*, p. 134.

82   Hansard, 'Springboks' Rugby Match, Swansea (Disturbances)', Monday 17 November 1969, https://api.parliament.uk/historic-hansard/commons/1969/nov/17/springboks-rugby-match-swansea

83   *Guardian*, 25 November 1969, p. http://specialbranchfiles.uk/anti-apartheid-movement-story/

84   See, for example, http://www.documentcloud.org/documents/2642491-1969-11-21-AAM-SB-Report.html

85   Peter Hain, *Radical Regeneration: Protest, Direct Action and Community Politics* (Quartet, 1975), p. 141.

86   'Inside Job', *Guardian*, 23 October 2002.

87   'Springbok protest "biggest success" of tour so far', *Guardian*, 24 November 1969; Hain, *Don't Play with Apartheid*, pp. 136-37; see also Bob Light's report highlighting police and fascist violence for *Socialist Worker*, 27 November 1969.

88   'Talks condemn tour', *Liverpool Guild Gazette* 25 November 1969, https://senatehouseoccupation.wordpress.com/1969/11/25/talks-condemn-tour-2/

89   *Manchester Evening News*, 26 November 1969, p. 1. See also *Morning Star*, 27 November 1969.

90   Janet Whelan, email communication with Geoff Brown, 9 May 2019.

91   Pete Halstead, 'Springboks - rugger off!', *Solidarity North West*, syndicalist magazine, vol 1, no.2, n.d., early 1970. Cockcroft used his middle name, Halstead, for the article.

92   *Daily Telegraph*, 27 November 1969, p. 1.

93   *The Times*, 27 November 1969.

94   See 'List of Complaints against Police Activities on Wednesday 26th November 1969'. University of Manchester Library, archive SEC/69/60

95   For more on Manchester, see Geoff Brown, 'Not just Peterloo: The Anti-Apartheid march to the Springbok match, Old Trafford, November 1969', *Socialist History* 56 (forthcoming).

96   Hain, *Don't Play with Apartheid*, pp. 138-39, and *Morning Star*, 3 December 1969. As Tony Collins notes, 'Aberdeen University's [rugby] club organised an alternative match that included black players on the day of the tourists' match against the North of Scotland'. Collins, *A Social History of English Rugby Union*, p. 180.

84 97   Sustar and Karim (eds.) *Poetry and Protest,* p. 136.

98   'February 11, 1970' http://razmatazmag.com/2016/february-11-1970/ Accessed 5 September 2019..

99   Personal information from Sally Kincaid and Jim Kincaid, 7 September 2019. See also Colin Barker, 'Audrey Farrell: Passionate about socialism', *Socialist Review* (February 2001) and 'Government's 30-year-old files reveal ugly side of Springboks tour that brought shame on our nation and Day John Lennon paid my demo fine', *The Herald,* 1 January 2001, online at https://www.heraldscotland.com/news/12157956.governments-30-year-old-files-reveal-ugly-side-of-springboks-tour-that-brought-shame-on-our-nation-day-john-lennon-paid-my-demo-fine/

100 Paul Holborow, conversation with Geoff Brown, 11 October 2019; Jeannie Robinson, conversation with Geoff Brown; Europe Singh, conversation with Geoff Brown, 25 October 2019.

101 *Morning Star,* 8 December 1969.

102 *Morning Star*, 8 December 1969.

103 *Morning Star*, 13 December 1969.

104 *Guardian*, 19th December 1969, p. 17.

105 Interview with Ernest Rodker (2013), https://www.aamarchives.org/file-view/file/7831-int21t-ernest-rodker.html

106 'Remembering bitter Springboks tour that paved a way for change', *Daily Telegraph*, 20 September 2006.

https://www.telegraph.co.uk/sport/rugbyunion/international/england/2346183/Remembering-bitter-Springboks-tour-that-paved-a-way-for-change.html

107 Hain, *Don't Play with Apartheid*, p. 142

108 Interview with Ernest Rodker (2013), https://www.aamarchives.org/file-view/file/7831-int21t-ernest-rodker.html

109 Ibid.

110 'Footnotes', *Private Eye*, 9 December 1969, p. 6.

111   Jim Nichol, email communication with Geoff Brown, August 2019.

112 Bob Newland interview with Geoff Brown, September 2019.

113 Bob Newland interview with Geoff Brown, September 2019. See also Ken Keable (ed.) *London Recruits: The Secret War against Apartheid* (Pontypool: The Merlin Press, 2012), p. 268. Thanks to Ken Keable for this reference.

114 Hain, *Don't Play with Apartheid*, p. 154.

115 Hain, *Outside In*, p. 56.

116 Hain, *Don't Play with Apartheid,* p. 144. For an overview of the Dublin protests in 1970, see '45 years ago: The controversial visit of the Springbok team to Dublin', *Come Here to Me!*, 3 February 2015, https://comeheretome.com/2015/02/03/45-years-ago-the-controversial-visit-of-the-springbok-team-to-dublin/

117 'Ulster may not play S. Africans', *Guardian*, 20 November 1969.

118 'Siege of the Springboks', *Irish Times*, 8 January 1970, p1.

119 *Free Citizen* No 5, November 1969.

120 *Free Citizen* No 13, January 1970.

121 *Irish Times*, 12 January 1970.

122 'Protests continue late into night', *Irish Press*, 12 January 1970; 'Batons used on hotel attackers', *Irish Times*, 12 January 1970, Michael Farrell in conversation with Geoff Brown, 16 September 2019.

123 Hain, *Don't Play with Apartheid*, p. 195.

124 Hain, *Don't Play with Apartheid* p. 173. See also Brearley, *On Cricket*, p. 130.

125 Michael Brearley, *On Form*, (London: Constable, 2018), pp. 18-19.

126 Hain, *Don't Play with Apartheid*, p. 172.

127 Hain, *Don't Play with Apartheid*, p. 177.

128 Interview with Jack Jones by Christabel Gurney (2013), AAM Archive, Bodleian Library, online at https://www.aamarchives.org/archive/interviews/jack-jones/into8t-jack-jones.html

129 Gurney, 'In the heart of the beast: The British Anti-Apartheid Movement, 1959–1994'

130 Hain, *Don't Play with Apartheid*, p.104.

131 Peter Hain, *Outside In* (London, Biteback Publishing, 2012), p. 63.

132 Hain, *Don't Play with Apartheid*, p. 163.

133 Stuart Hall, Chas Critcher, Tony Jefferson, John Clarke and Brian Roberts, *Policing the Crisis: Mugging, the State and Law and Order* (Basingstoke: Macmillan, 1978), pp. 251-252, and Hain, *Don't Play with Apartheid*, p. 152

134 https://socialistworker.co.uk/art/2675/When+Swansea++mauled+racism+

135 Hain, *Don't Play with Apartheid* p. 166.

136 Hain, *Don't Play with Apartheid* p. 168.

137 Hain, *Don't Play Against Apartheid*, p. 175.

138 Elizabeth M Williams, *The Politics of Race in Britain and South Africa: Black British Solidarity and the Anti-Apartheid Struggle* (London, I.B. Taurus, 2017), p. 127.

139 Hain, *Don't Play with Apartheid*, p. 174.

140 Hain, *Don't Play with Apartheid*, p. 201.

141 'Police cheer move to stop Springbok tour', *Times*, 22 May 1979.

142 *The Times*, 23 May 1970.

143 Christabel Gurney, personal information, 7 October 2019.

144 Hain, *Don't Play with Apartheid*, p. 195.

145 Hain, *Outside In*, p. 66.

146 Peter Oborne, *Basil D'Oliveira*, p. 252.

147 Quoted in Booth, 'Hitting Apartheid for Six?' p. 480.

148 Pendry, *Taking It on the Chin*, p.254.

149 *Morning Star*, 18 December 1969.

150 Hain, *Sing the Beloved Country*, p. 55.

151 Hain, *Outside In*, pp56-57.

152 Hain, *Outside In*, pp. 65-66.

153 'Rugby family has shameful past in propping up apartheid regime', *Irish Times*, 10 December 2013.

https://www.irishtimes.com/sport/rugby/rugby-family-has-shameful-past-in-propping-up-apartheid-regime-1.1622452

154 'Remembering bitter Springboks tour that paved a way for change', *Daily Telegraph*, 20 September 2006. https://www.telegraph.co.uk/sport/rugbyunion/international/england/2346183/Remembering-bitter-Springboks-tour-that-paved-a-way-for-change.html

155 'How Siya Kolisi's Springboks brought hope to troubled South Africa', *Independent*, 3 November 2019, https://www.independent.co.uk/sport/rugby/rugby-union/international/rugby-world-cup-2019-south-africa-siya-kolisi-erasmus-race-unity-springboks-a9182671.html For a more critical analysis of the contemporary inequalities still scarring the Springboks, see Allan Hendricks, 'SA Rugby's transformation problem', *New Frame*, 28 October 2019, https://www.newframe.com/sa-rugbys-transformation-problem/

156 Ronnie Kasrils, personal communication to Geoff Brown, 4 November 2019.

25 YEARS AFTER APARTHEID, SOUTHERN AFRICA STILL NEEDS OUR SOLIDARITY

partner with ACTSA to deliver rights, equality and sustainable development

"Eradicating the legacy of apartheid
and rebuilding our region will take many years.
We need your support and we warmly welcome
the transformation of the Anti-Apartheid Movement to
Action for Southern Africa"
Nelson Mandela

for more information
actsa.org/get-involved

Anti-Apartheid Movement Archives

'Forward to Freedom' is an online archive telling the story of the British Anti-Apartheid Movement, 1959–1994

It features posters, leaflets and documents from the AAM and sister organisations like the International Defence and Aid Fund (IDAF), Namibia Support Committee and Committee for Freedom in Mozambique, Angola and Guiné.

If you have memorabilia from anti-apartheid campaigns or memories you would like to share, please contact us.

AAM Archives has a pop-up exhibition available for free loan to educational and community organisations (22 x A2 boards).

We are also part of LACE (Learning from anti-apartheid campaigns through a community of education), a coalition which produces resources for schools about anti-apartheid solidarity and its relevance to campaigns against racism and inequality today.

Contact: info@aamarchives.org
www.aamarchives.org

AAM ARCHIVES

APARTHEID IS NOT A GAME

Jerry Dammers in *Reminiscences of RAR*

I probably responded to Rock Against Racism partly because I had been involved in anti-racism from years before, when I had campaigned against Apartheid, specifically against the South African Springboks' rugby tour which was the first demonstration I ever went on, when I was about fifteen. I had put stickers around the school and managed to recruit a posse of about two others to come on the demonstration. An old school friend maybe remembered that when years later in 1983 I met him in the street and he told me about a concert at Alexander [sic] Palace celebrating the 65th birthday of someone I had never heard of - Nelson Mandela. The anti-racist theme influenced by Rock Against Racism continued after the Fun Boy Three had left the Specials, when I wrote my song Free Nelson Mandela, inspired by a song Julian Bahula sang about Mandela, which I heard at that Alexander Palace concert. My song then became known around the world. That in turn led to Dali Tambo, the son of the leader of the ANC Oliver Tambo, asking me to organise Artists Against Apartheid in Britain. We held a series of concerts, based to an extent on the Rock Against Racism model, and that sense of concerts grew into the largest Anti-Apartheid demonstration ever held anywhere at the time the 200 thousand strong Clapham Common concert in 1986. That in turn led to the two Wembley Stadium Mandela concerts that were seen by millions of people around the world. I think it is highly likely all that would not have happened in the way it did, if it hadn't been for the inspiration, success, and not to mention the support, of Rock Against Racism, That organisation and Red Saunders, as well as the Anti-Nazi League do deserve a share in some of whatever credit may be due for all that stuff happening in Britain.

a Redwords book

REMINISCENCES OF RAR: Rocking Against Racism 1976-1982

Edited by Roger Huddle & Red Saunders
+ 70 contributors
2nd expanded edition Spring 2020